Patrick Regan is the founder and CEO ⟨
poverty, supports education and helps yo
He recently won the Mayor of London's p
Soul Survivor and Spring Harvest, and is a frequent guest ᴏɴ ʀᴀᴅᴵᴏ
TV programmes. He is also an Ambassador for Compassion.

Liza Hoeksma is a freelance writer.

* * *

"Recent history shows us that hope is the real 'X' factor that everyone needs in life. Patrick offers us no hollow clichés or quick fixes, but breathtakingly honest, practical gems that emerge from his life and work. Read this page turner, be inspired by its faith-filled authenticity, and catch the spirit of hope that keeps the world changers going. Brilliant and refreshing."
– Jeff Lucas, author, speaker, broadcaster

"This amazingly hopeful manifesto for change is earth-shaking. Reading this book will get you ready."
– Danielle Strickland, author, *The Liberating Truth*

"This is the future of the church, found amongst those others consider hopeless. Forget door knocking to tell people about Jesus, XLP loves like Jesus – and the press and politicians knock on their door to ask for the hope that they have."
– Jarrod McKenna, Australian peace award recipient and co-founder of The Peace Tree Community

"This is a book for those who long for change on our city streets, and in the neediest places in the world. Patrick combines biblical faith and ground level experience to show that change is possible, when it is rooted in hope."
– Rt Revd Graham Cray, Archbishops' Missioner and Chairman of the Soul Survivor Trust

"Patrick is an incredible visionary. This powerful book reminds us all that there is no ceiling to God's ability to transform a community. You'll walk away from it dreaming bigger and believing God's kingdom can impact your town and your streets."
– Vicky Beeching, worship leader and blogger

"In the face of growing unrest across the globe, incivility that staggers human decency and deflates our confidence in the common good, Patrick Regan offers a sober, yet hopeful response. With over fifteen years' experience on the front lines of London's inner-city landscape, Regan knows the challenges all too well, but also taps into the unlimited potential of the One who can transform the heart and restore the city."

– Louie Giglio, Pastor, Passion City Church and Passion Conferences, Atlanta

"Patrick Regan is a prophet. He finds diamonds in the mud... This has some of the most thrilling stories you'll ever read of the transforming power of Jesus. Don't just buy one copy, but get another and give it to a friend who is not yet a Christian. It'll show them why we get so excited about Jesus."

– Eric Delve, St Luke's Church, Maidstone

" Patrick puts his hands on the ugliness of our world and squeezes out huge portions of hope. This isn't a book about wishful thinking; it's a book about God at work in a broken world."

– Revd Joel Edwards, International Director, Micah Challenge

"Explores the life-giving force of hope. Written directly to all of us who claim to love Jesus, Patrick courageously exposes his own fragile vulnerability in order to help us more effectively understand what it really means to live as a Christian."

– Diane Louise Jordan, TV presenter

"Patrick is a man on a mission. Whether on the streets of London or in a developing country on the other side of the world he is committed to serving others and to helping to change people's lives and circumstances. This book is moving and inspiring and cannot fail to challenge all who read it."

– Revd Les Isaac, founder, Street Pastors

NO CEILING TO HOPE

STORIES OF GRACE IN ACTION FROM THE WORLD'S MOST DANGEROUS PLACES

PATRICK REGAN

WITH LIZA HOEKSMA

MONARCH
BOOKS

Oxford, UK & Grand Rapids, Michigan, USA

First published in the UK in 2012 by Monarch Books (a publishing imprint of Lion Hudson plc) and by Elevation (a publishing imprint of the Memralife Group):
Lion Hudson plc, Wilkinson House, Jordan Hill Road, Oxford OX2 8DR
Tel: +44 (0)1865 302750; Fax +44 (0)1865 302757;
email monarch@lionhudson.com; www.lionhudson.com
Memralife Group, 14 Horsted Square, Uckfield, East Sussex TN22 1QG
Tel: +44 (0)1825 746530; Fax +44 (0)1825 748899; www.elevationmusic.com

ISBN 978 0 85721 222 1 (print)
ISBN 978 0 85721 282 5 (epub)
ISBN 978 0 85721 281 8 (Kindle)
ISBN 978 0 85721 283 2 (PDF)

Distributed by:
UK: Marston Book Services, PO Box 269, Abingdon, Oxon OX14 4YN
USA: Kregel Publications, PO Box 2607, Grand Rapids, Michigan 49501

British Library Cataloguing Data
A catalogue record for this book is available from the British Library.

Printed and bound in Great Britain by Clays Ltd, St Ives plc

To Simon & Ali:
Your support, love and
commitment to Diane and me,
and to XLP, have kept us going.
You're both an inspiration.
Patrick

Contents

Foreword

No *Ceiling to Hope* is for such a time as this. It will inform you, challenge you, break – and warm – your heart.

Some of the stories in these pages are truly shocking and could easily lead to a sense of despair about what is happening in our world today. Addiction, wars, gangs, poverty and pain, homelessness and hunger.

Yet Patrick constantly gives us stories of hope, courage, love and triumph. He's been into many of the world's darkest places, but has found that God's people are there bringing light. He's visited places of brokenness and seen first hand those servants who are willingly mending things in God's name. Much of the work being done isn't glamorous and won't get talked about on the world stage, but it's absolutely vital work for God's church, part of the reason for her very existence.

Likewise the work being done by Patrick and his team at XLP. From Peckham to Jamaica, from Tower Hamlets to Ghana they are pouring out their hearts and lives in the service of those who, to the uninitiated, may seem to be the most undeserving. Patrick and his friends have seen beneath the surface and have touched the despair of a generation who have never felt loved, affirmed or accepted: a generation often without hope. The team are ordinary, vulnerable people and God is using them to pour his healing and grace into these broken lives.

This book presents a challenge to each one of us to follow their example, to hear God's call for us to stand up for the marginalized and oppressed, and to do everything we can to bring heaven to earth. We as the church can bring hope and transformation to a world in desperate need – if we will only act. And, as Patrick is so right in saying, we do this most effectively in the strength of Jesus who is himself the hope of the world.

Patrick has been my good friend for many years now. I have watched the ministry of XLP grow and develop and at the same time not lose its heart, vulnerability and passion. XLP is an authentic ministry from authentic people who have too much integrity to enlarge their stories of grace. I am confident that what you read here is absolutely reliable. They are the real deal. I have seen the suffering and the days of despair over the years and Patrick doesn't shy away from honest accounts of his own struggles. But I have also seen the provision and mercy of God poured out in the most amazing ways and the miracles God has done through Patrick's obedience.

The stories you find here will move you. But be warned they don't make for comfortable bedtime reading: they will inspire you to love, to act, to serve and to pour yourself out to bring the hope our world so desperately needs.

Finally, I love Patrick dearly. I am so proud of him. I commend this man and his book to you with all my heart.

Mike Pilavachi
December 2011

Acknowledgments

Special thanks to Diane, Keziah, Daniel and Abigail. I have been privileged to travel to so many places mentioned in this book only because you have been so releasing of me. I am humbled by your constant love and support.

Liza – I love working with you; it's always full of lots of laughter and then some tears.

Thanks to all those who helped out with stories and input: Simon Marchant, Johnny and Catherine Smith, Margaret Ferguson and those at Woodvale Church in the Shankhill community, Emily Vesey, Adrian and Jane, Andy Flanagan, Mike Biddulph, Becca Brierley, Dad, Leanne Sedin, Tom Booker and Mike Coates.

Special thanks to some of my heroes: Akousa Arkhurst, the students at Jubilee School and all my friends in Ghana; and Ms Lorna Stanley and Debbie in Trenchtown. I have told your stories many times, as you are real examples of what loving the hell out of people looks like.

Thanks to those who offered so much help and support in getting this book done: Wendy Beech-Ward, Tony Collins, Jenny Ward, Phil Loose, Ian Hamilton and all those at Compassion, Ibiere Oruwari and my amazing PA, Becky Hunt.

The XLP team: it's a real privilege to lead such an amazing bunch of people who are so committed to seeing change happen from the grass-roots up.

About XLP

started the charity XLP after a stabbing in a school over fifteen years ago. I had no idea what I could do to help when the school approached me – I just knew I was called to do something.

I had grown up in Chelmsford and had only recently become a youth worker in a church in London. As I got to know these young people, I began to see what many of them faced every day of their lives: broken homes, financial and emotional poverty, educational failure, and living in areas where gangs, drugs and crime were becoming an increasingly significant problem. Many of these young people were becoming "outcasts" – from their schools, from their families and from society.

The longer I worked with them, the more my heart broke for them. I could see all the potential that God had given them to be amazing people and live incredible lives, and at the same time I could see them struggling against so many issues. I knew I had to stand with them – live, laugh and cry with them – and that God had called me to follow Jesus' example in embracing the least, the last and the lost amongst the young people of London.

It has been a hugely challenging journey. From working with a few kids in a single school, XLP has grown to now work in over sixty schools across seven inner-London boroughs and in numerous estate communities, reaching 12,000 young people every year through schools and after-schools clubs, a double-decker bus project, a "pimped out" police riot van, art showcases, sports coaching and our mentoring programme. We run a gap-year training programme called Experience, which works in partnership with local churches, and we also partner with St Mellitus College to offer a degree course in theology and youth ministry. We have built a school in Ghana, and worked with people in Bangladesh, China, Turkey, Jamaica, South Africa and so many other places around the world. The stories along the way have been a combination of elation and tragedy. We've seen many find hope for the future in what seemed like hopeless situations. We've even had young people we work with become volunteers and staff members at XLP.

You can read more about the history of XLP in the book *Conspiracy of the Insignificant* (Kingsway, 2007). You can also read more about gang culture and why young people are drawn to it in my book *Fighting Chance* (Hodder, 2010).

If you're interested in finding out more about the work of XLP, or you would like to volunteer, donate or get involved in one of our projects, we'd love to hear from you. You can contact us in the following ways:

- Website: www.xlp.org.uk
- Postal address: 12 Belmont Hill, Lewisham, London SE13 5BD
- Telephone: 020 8297 8284
- Email: info@xlp.org.uk

You can also find us on:

- YouTube: www.youtube.com/xlplondon
- Facebook: www.facebook.com/xlplondon
- Twitter: www.twitter.com/xlplondon and www.twitter.com/PatrickReganXLP

Chapter 1
The Chance of Hope

London, October 2009. Ben, a thirty-year-old man, walks home from a nightclub with his girlfriend Allana, after an evening celebrating her birthday. Three young men stumble across them and grab Allana's fancy dress hat from her head. When she asks for it back, the youths punch her, then attack Ben, hitting him in the face and pushing him to the ground. As he lies helpless, they violently kick his head, inflicting such serious wounds that Ben dies just a few hours later from catastrophic brain damage. CCTV cameras capture delight on the young men's faces as they stand over Ben's broken body.[1]

A year later, as the offending men were put on trial and sentenced, I was invited to talk on a national TV station about this tragic incident as an example of the growing violence amongst young people. The topic was pretty grim. The news had been full of reports of the increasing brutality amongst the UK's young people. Teenagers killing each other over anything from a look they didn't like, to the fact that the victim lived in a postcode they didn't like. Young people were also responsible for many deaths of innocent bystanders like Ben; lives were being lost over nothing more than a hat, leaving families and communities devastated at the senseless deaths.

As I sat there nervously on the plush studio sofa, I talked to the TV presenters as we waited for our cue. They took a polite interest in the work I do in inner-city London and around the world, but their weariness was written all over their faces.

They'd seen too much. Gathering and reporting the news for a number of years had exposed them to the escalation of futile gang wars, story after story of young people becoming increasingly violent, volatile, and involved in serious crime. The female presenter shook her head as she said there was only one conclusion to draw from the evidence: this was a lost generation. My heart fell to the floor. Here I was, planning to talk about how we could help young people, see past the labels and stereotypes, choose not to write kids off when they've never been given a chance in life; and the people interviewing me could see no possible future for this entire generation. How many of the viewers thought the exact same thing? What did it mean for young people if adults were ready to write them off?

As the cameras started rolling and the red light shone, telling me we were live on air, my mind was scrambling around trying to think of the best way to address this lack of hope. The picture was bleak; that I couldn't disagree with. There was no doubt about it, things were bad and seemed to be getting worse. I saw it every day in my work: young people were getting into drug dealing to make some easy money. They were dropping out of school and becoming increasingly isolated from society. They were angry and frustrated and saw violence as their only form of expression. But despite all of that, despite working day in and day out with these young people who were struggling, and despite being all too aware of what they were facing, I couldn't agree with the presenter's conclusion. I locked eyes with this woman who thought there was no hope for this generation of young people and said, "I refuse to believe this is a lost generation. I am convinced that if we tackle the drivers of why these things happen, we can bring about change. Hope is a refusal to accept a situation as it is."

As Christians, hope is an amazing part of our heritage and our inheritance. It can set us apart and make us stand out in a society that is increasingly cynical and worn down by the pain it sees in the world today. We worship the God of all hope (Romans 15:13), the God who clearly demonstrates to us through the Bible that there is always reason to have hope, no matter how bad things seem. This has never been clearer than when we look to Jesus dying on the cross. We barely need reminding of what a dark day it was for Jesus' followers as they saw their leader publicly humiliated and brutally beaten. For the Jewish people standing there on Good Friday, it was a catastrophe and a moment when their dreams were crushed and hope seemed futile. God's chosen people had experienced the oppression of overlord nations such as the Assyrians, the Babylonians, the Medo-Persians, and the Greeks over several hundred years. At the time of Jesus, they were being ruled over by the Romans. Many of the Jewish people, particularly the poor, were beleaguered and worn down. All they wanted was to be left to rule their own land; to have God's land inhabited and ruled by God's people without interference. Instead they were being oppressed by yet another ruling enemy. The Romans may have let them keep their own customs to some degree, but they had to pay extortionate taxes and they were living in fear, knowing that those who didn't obey and co-operate would be easily disposed of. All they had to cling to was the hope of the promises of God.

That hope had been passed from generation to generation as they waited. And waited. And waited. But they believed God would be true to his word and a Messiah would come to restore their kingdom. They weren't entirely sure whether this Messiah would be a king, a prophet, a priest or a warrior, but from the way they reacted to Jesus, it seems they were hoping for a warrior who would step in and overturn the powerful Roman Empire. They wanted a revolution. They wanted Jerusalem and Israel to return to the glories of the time of King David and King

Solomon. No doubt they had visions of God's armies marching towards Jerusalem, hopes that their longings would be fulfilled and their nation would be great again. Then along came Jesus; they thought he might be the Messiah, but he didn't seem to be acting like a warrior king. They watched events unfold and saw him arrested, convicted and executed brutally and publicly. When they looked at Jesus hanging naked, beaten, alone and seemingly humiliated on the cross, any remaining hopes of him being the Messiah must have been shattered. He wasn't evicting the pagan Romans who tainted their land, restoring their nation to its former glory or ushering in Yahweh's return to the Temple. He was being cursed, nailed to a Roman cross and killed like a criminal. Public humiliation and death; what a dark day for Jesus' followers.

For all those whose hopes had rested with him, it looked as if the Romans had won again. Their hopes had come to nothing and Jesus had failed to fulfil their dreams. So the mockers looked on and laughed. The Romans may have sat back and thought they had stamped out this upstart carpenter from Galilee. Many of Jesus' disciples fell into disarray and desperately tried to make sense of what was going on and decide what to do. It looked like an absolute disaster, but even in those dark moments, there was reason to hope. As we well know, God was up to something. In that desperate and bleak situation, God was actually working for the salvation of all humankind. Jesus' followers had been right to put their hope in him, right to trust that God would be true to his word. The cross is the ultimate example of the fact that things aren't always what they seem, that God can work for good in any situation and that with God there is always reason to hope.

Perspective

Hope calls into question the present reality. It may seem as if hope is illusive sometimes but it's a choice about what perspective you choose to take. If you walk along the street and look down at the ground, you often focus on the grey concrete slabs. They are dirty and depressing, lifeless and miserable. But if you look harder you might see something else. Anywhere there is a gap between the concrete slabs there are signs of life. Grass will fight its way up, desperate to get to the surface, craning and straining against the odds to grow up towards the light. You can slap concrete on the ground but you can't keep life down. There's always something growing and looking for life, something surviving despite the odds.

That's what this book is all about: facing up to the reality that often life looks like a series of concrete slabs, and learning to focus our gaze on where the grass is growing, where hope is springing into life, where Christians are bringing God's life and love and seeing change. We'll look at the fact that even if you try to pull the grass up, you'll find that its roots are still there and new shoots will start to grow. We'll be looking at where we get our hope from, the true and unending hope that is ours in Jesus. We'll be challenging ourselves to see hope where the world sees disaster, to cling on to hope till our dying breath, to find evidence for hope when confronted with pain and misery. We'll be looking at one of the key challenges for us as Christians today: how do we gain and keep a perspective of hope, no matter what? We'll be looking at God's perspective, which comes from a place of hope, where love can overcome hate, where forgiveness can overcome bitterness, brokenness and violence. We'll be looking at how we stay in it for the long haul, not letting our spirits be dampened but understanding that if we make this our life's work, we'll eventually see the grass breaking through the concrete and taking over the landscape.

We have to train ourselves to have this perspective of hope, because when we talk about the state of the world it's easy to focus on the negative things. We're constantly told how bad things are, but if you're anything like me, the statistics quoted are so huge that it's hard to wrap your head around them and make them mean something. How can we visualize the 1.1 billion people who don't have access to safe drinking water?[2] Or the 8 million children whose lives could have been saved if their parents had access to the right medicine?[3] We look at the massive numbers and it's hard to imagine that things can ever change, that we can make any difference at all. We feel like a tiny ant trying to move a mighty oak tree. If we're going to bring change, we have to have hope for what we can achieve. So let's start by looking at some of the signs of life and some of the statistics of amazing change. It seems to be one of today's best-kept secrets that there is good stuff happening in our world, and not just small changes in individuals and communities (though these are crucially important and something I want to talk a lot about). There are also enormous, wonderful and world-altering changes happening that are the rewards reaped from people's compassion and dedication to stamping out pain and suffering where they can. Change is happening:

- The number of people living in extreme poverty has been halved in the last 30 years (from 52 per cent of the world's population to 26 per cent).
- Whilst 40,000 children used to die every day from preventable causes, that figure now stands at 21,000.
- 22 countries have halved their rates of malaria in 6 years.

- The number of children dying from measles has dropped by 78 per cent in the last 8 years.[4]

Now *that* motivates me. In my lifetime alone, the number of people living in extreme poverty has halved. Halved! I hope to have at least as many years ahead of me as there are behind me, so what else could I expect to see happen? What else could we achieve? What disease could we wipe out? What social injustice could we obliterate? What legacy could we leave that would have future generations looking back at the early twenty-first century and saying, "Wow, those people wouldn't stop. They worked tirelessly on their watch. No one thought it could be done but they changed the world."

Hope without limits

Clearly, it isn't just Christians who are involved in trying to end poverty, injustice and suffering in this world, so why does the church need to get involved when there are so many amazing organizations doing great work?

The first and most obvious answer is that God calls us to do these things and to be his hands and feet in this world.

The second answer is that as God's people we have something amazing and unique to offer the world: hope without limit. He gives us hope for today, that things can change in the here and now. But he also gives us hope for eternity, the promise of a day when every tear will be wiped away and everything will be restored. We have both hope for eternal life and hope that God cares right here and right now. He's not the strange old man in the sky who only takes an interest in us after death – and then only to invite us into paradise or send us off to eternal damnation. Who wants to be in relationship with someone like that? Our God cares; he cares enough to embrace the sin of the world on the cross. He cares enough to come and get involved, he cares enough to say, "I want to help you out of your brokenness, poverty and pain." He screams throughout the Bible that he can't bear injustice, that he wants his people to be compassionate and care for the poor. His very essence is love and he sums up his entire law in saying: love God, *and* love your neighbour as yourself.

The third answer is that the church is uniquely positioned to deliver things other organizations can't. The church is made up of millions and millions of people worldwide, with congregations placed all over the globe. Whilst some relief efforts are hampered by corrupt governments and local officials who steal or redistribute aid for their own benefit, churches are often ideally placed to get aid to where it is most needed.

Even people outside of the church acknowledge that it has a lot to offer. In an article in *The Times* entitled "As an atheist, I truly believe Africa needs God", Matthew Parris describes the difference that he believes the Christian faith makes:

> *Now a confirmed atheist, I've become convinced of the enormous contribution that Christian evangelism makes in Africa: sharply distinct from the work of secular NGOs, government projects and international aid efforts. These alone will not do. Education and training alone will not do. In Africa Christianity changes people's hearts. It brings a spiritual transformation. The rebirth is real. The change is good...*
>
> *I would allow that if faith was needed to motivate missionaries to help, then, fine: but what counted was the help, not the faith. But this*

doesn't fit the facts. Faith does more than support the missionary; it is also transferred to his flock. This is the effect that matters so immensely, and which I cannot help observing...

Whenever we entered a territory worked by missionaries, we had to acknowledge that something changed in the faces of the people we passed and spoke to: something in their eyes, the way they approached you direct, man-to-man, without looking down or away.[5]

Culturally engaged but morally distinct

Sometimes it can seem as though it would be an easier task to go to some far-flung place to deliver aid and preach the gospel, and far more of a challenge to do it on our own doorsteps. Why? Because the Western church seems perhaps to be in a time of exile. Belief in Christian values is being eroded, religion and society are no longer in sync, and the church is often seen as an outdated, irrelevant or even dangerous institution. Schools no longer sing hymns, many find it an offence to celebrate Christmas and would rather call it the "Winter Festival".

The people of God have found themselves in a state of exile many times throughout history. When the Babylonian army invaded and destroyed Jerusalem, the people of God were taken into exile. Tens of thousands of Hebrews were herded across several hundred miles of desert to live in a new place where Yahweh was unknown. There was no Temple of God, no Levitical sacrifices, no Yahwistic festivals and celebrations, and a wholly different set of values. Put simply, they were "aliens in a foreign land" and they felt it. The book of Lamentations expresses the crushing sadness they felt; they were a people who felt abandoned, rootless, vulnerable and orphaned. Yet in that place, and with that sense of vulnerability, God told them through Jeremiah:

> *This is what the Lord Almighty, the God of Israel, says to all those I carried into exile from Jerusalem to Babylon: "Build houses and settle down; plant gardens and eat what they produce... Also, seek the peace and prosperity of the city to which I have carried you into exile. Pray to the Lord for it..."*
>
> **Jeremiah 29:4–7**

The Jews were free to build houses, earn a living wage and observe their customs and religion, but they couldn't return home to their capital. At the same time, they were called to be different by the prophets of old and to maintain the integrity of their identity as Yahweh's chosen people, even in their current circumstances. That was the tension they had to hold to, and that is what we need to rediscover today.

The key thing for us to remember, whenever we are confronted with the challenge of being a church in exile, is that we have several choices about how we respond. We can fight the change from Christmas to "Winterval"; we can sign petitions and complain loudly to anyone who will listen. Sometimes there is a place for all of that and it's important to stand up for what we believe in, but does it help people hear our message and turn towards our God? Our second choice is to batten down the hatches, hide ourselves away and create a Christian subculture that exists behind walls. We can have a view of mission that's akin to scurrying out of our safe-house once a year to capture anyone who doesn't put up a fight and dragging them back with us. Then we can make them into clones of ourselves, only able to survive in a Christian bubble. Thirdly, we can choose to embrace living in "Babylon", go along with its culture and live by its values because, let's face it, life's a lot less hassle that way. We can blend in, become synonymous with our surroundings, periodically telling stories of the old days but treating them more like fairy tales than inspiration to live by. We can forget our past, forget who we are and what our story is. *GQ* magazine wrote a feature about evangelical Christians, which woefully concluded that we are essentially a Xerox copy of the wider culture – not markedly different in any way.[6]

Or there's another choice. We can stand up and stand out in our world. We can stand for something different. We have the dangerous stories of Jesus to drive our hope. We can follow his example and turn from today's culture of consumerism, greed and selfish living. We need to check whether our values are too in line with the world around us. Maybe we're trying to be culturally relevant, or maybe we just like living in nice houses, driving nice cars, planning our careers, and buying our kids the latest trends. Maybe we've bought into the culture of individualism. Even within the church we more often ask, "What is *my* calling?" than, "What is *our* calling as the body of Christ?"

We need to remember that we're meant to be distinctive. We are not here to keep the government, our friends, our colleagues or anyone else happy: we are here to serve the kingdom of God. Which means sometimes people will love us and other times they won't understand us at all. So instead of being distracted by false idols like success, money, fame and security, we should be facing up to the problems and challenges in our communities and around the world and finding new ways of engaging with them. We need to take ownership of the problems around us and work with people who are suffering in order to find solutions. Wouldn't that make people take notice for the best possible reasons? Wouldn't that pique their interest in God if they saw his people were carrying such hope that they kept on going, believing there can be lasting change, and were prepared to make sacrifices themselves to see it happen?

Stories of hope

During their time in exile the Israelites recalled their history and the stories of what God had done in the past. I think of these as dangerous stories of grace in action, and they are just as important for us today as they were for the Israelites. These stories inspired the people of God. They were daring, unsettling and even scary, but they would fill God's people with courage. Telling these stories of God's goodness and his plan for the whole of creation brings us hope today. We have the same stories as the Israelites had, of a God who parted the Red Sea, who rained down food from heaven, who brought water out from a rock. We can also tell of a carpenter from Nazareth who healed the sick, raised the dead, loved the poor and the disenfranchised, and set the captives free. We have stories of how Jesus saw and met with individuals. How he met with a woman abused by men and scorned by her society, and gave her dignity for today and hope for tomorrow. How he encountered a man with leprosy, healing him and setting him free from the stigma that had dominated his life and determined his future. We have stories of a Saviour who is all about forgiveness and restoration. Every time we remember how he embraced a child everyone else thought was a waste of time, we are shown a glimpse of God's intentions for human history, a foretaste of the future with God. We're reminded we have a God who cares, who gets involved; we have a God who loves.

This is the activity of the King; this is the work of the kingdom, an indication of what is to come. This is what the church is called to do. Rather than simply hanging around on earth, doing our own thing in our own way, and waiting to die and "go to heaven", our God has called us to partner with him in realizing his ultimate purposes of recreating heaven and earth to be all that he intends it to be. That's huge! The all-powerful Creator of the universe who formed the stars and our world and all life, loves you and me and wants us to become all that he intends us to be by working with him towards the re-imagining of heaven and earth! When we work with God like this, towards his ultimate goal and purpose, we are changed, the people and the world around us change too, and every now and again we see a glimpse of what it will be like when we walk with God in the restored universe. On this journey we are not only echoing the dangerous stories of the past, but becoming intimately involved in those stories that God is writing upon history today.

At XLP we meet as a team every Monday morning and one of the most important things we do is share dangerous stories of change as they happen. Sometimes the stories make us laugh, other times they bring us to tears. They fill us with the courage and compassion to keep going with the things God has set before us. When we see God break into a young person's life, we are encouraged and reminded that this is God's will. When we see a family restored, their lives put back together, we're reminded that this is the kingdom come on earth. We tell and retell the stories, making sure that all our volunteers hear them – and as many other people as possible. Stories have the power to inspire, to break your heart, to make you laugh, to make you cry, to fill you with courage and compassion, to galvanize you into action. They prompt faith, hope and action, provoke change and challenge complacency. They remind us we are a community of people gathered around a cause, not a social club or a self-help meeting.

In this book I want to share some of the stories of where I've seen hope in our world. I've seen some terrifying and desperately painful situations transformed by God's people getting involved and bringing a piece of heaven to earth. As God's people we have an amazing opportunity to constantly evolve the story. There are so many areas that can be seen as lost causes, but as God's people we need to have a different perspective. God challenges us to see the world through his eyes. If we believe he can make any difference in our world, then we need to start seeing things in a new way. When others are giving up and calling a situation "hopeless", shouldn't we be standing firm, calling on the promises of God, refusing to accept a situation as it is, and being fully persuaded that there is *always* hope?

Chapter 2
Hope in Bolivia

I have been to a number of places around the world where people live in extreme poverty, but nothing I had encountered before prepared me for the things I saw in Bolivia. I'd been invited by the child development organization, Compassion, which is fairly well known in Christian circles, particularly for their child sponsorship programme. They took me to Bolivia to meet some of the families they work with and see first-hand what daily life is like for some of the 10 million people living in one of South America's poorest countries. The country itself is beautiful, with a backdrop of incredible snow-capped mountains and some of the most picturesque lakes you could ever see. Sadly, the stunning postcard pictures don't tell the full story of this country that has been left in poverty after many wars and much political instability.

One of the first families I encountered was a woman and her seven children, whom we visited in their small one-roomed mud hut. The family slept in just one bed and there was room for very little else in their home. The kitchen was a single gas stove with a few blackened pots and pans. As we sat together on the bed (it was the only place to sit), I asked about their life.

Often when I meet new people in these situations they are really keen to share their experiences with me and quickly open up about the struggles and reality of their daily life. This family were different; they clearly didn't want to revisit the painful memories of their past.

So we started talking about general issues that people around them were dealing with. One huge problem in any poor country is malnutrition, and this is common in Bolivia, where they have the second highest infant mortality rate in Latin America. Often it's something that's totally preventable like diarrhoea or a respiratory infection that proves fatal to a child whose body is weakened through their poor diet. Most of the countries I've been to where people are living in terrible conditions have a hot climate. In Bolivia, it may be quite warm during the day but the temperatures regularly drop to below freezing in the winter, and the family told me people there have very few ways to protect themselves against the cold. They said it's common for six kids to share the same bed with their parents and this can lead to lots of abusive situations. We were told that men in the households (fathers and uncles) frequently drink heavily because they are so desperate to forget all that's going on around them. This, of course, takes its toll on the rest of the family and uses up vital funds, but it's hard to judge someone for trying to block out their pain in such horrendous conditions.

As we talked, the family gradually began to open up and tell me a bit about their own lives. I found out that all the children worked; there was no other option to try to feed everyone. The oldest ones started at 5 a.m., taking a shift before school, then came home after school to look after the youngest siblings so their mum could do her job. As I sat talking to the woman, the deep sadness etched into her face and the weariness of her posture told me she'd been through more than I could imagine. With tears in her eyes, she told me that when she had realized she was pregnant with her seventh child, her husband had killed himself. The thought of bringing another child into such poverty, of having another mouth to feed when they already had so little, was more than he could bear. So she was a widow, left alone with her grief and the daily issue of how to keep her family alive.

I left heavy-hearted, trying to get my head around this woman's life, only to find that our next visit to a family home was to give me one of the starkest views of poverty I have ever seen. The household set-up was similar to that seen throughout many parts of Bolivia, where three families lived in simple adjoining brick structures, sharing one toilet (with just a hanging tarpaulin sheet for a door) and a barrel of water. They also shared one open-air "kitchen" consisting of a makeshift stove made of bricks and wood, two gas rings and one blackened pot.

We visited a woman and her four children who shared a small living space and a single bed between them. This woman was so malnourished that after she had given birth to her twins she couldn't produce any breast milk to feed them. In desperation, she found the only thing she could afford to buy for them was dog food. My mouth hung open in shock. The two beautiful six-month-old babies bouncing on my knee were being fed like animals. It broke my heart and those of the workers from Compassion. I could see they were genuinely moved to tears even though I knew they encountered situations of such desperation all the time, and I couldn't help but admire them for it. When you see poverty on that sort of scale, or suffering of any kind, it's hard not to start to toughen up and let your heart grow hard. Some would even say it's sensible to shut down a little just so you can keep going. But these guys seemed to be following the example of Jesus and caring for people from a soft heart.

Jesus was moved by people's situations and sufferings and he didn't toughen up in order to keep going. He drew strength from his Father and kept his heart soft so that he was moved by people's suffering. I think that softness is key to keeping hope alive and keeping going in the face of such pain. Real Jesus-like compassion isn't about feeling sorry for people or getting emotional when you're watching something sad on TV; it's a gut-wrenching feeling that something needs to be done. It's allowing your heart to break, not so that you sit there feeling emotionally wrung out, but so that when the compassion is combined with hope, it leads to action. Sometimes we sing or pray about God breaking our hearts with the things that break his. To be honest, I'm not sure I could handle it if God truly showed me how much his heart breaks for the suffering in our world. I could barely handle the reality of these twins, knowing that even if we could help them there were thousands more like them in Bolivia and millions more around the world. How would my heart bear to carry even a fraction of the grief that God knows when he cares so much for each and every one of those children?

I asked the team at Compassion how they manage to work in the midst of such need and pain and not harden their hearts. They told me the only way they can do it is by sticking close to God. They take comfort from knowing God is able to change any situation, no matter how desperate or hopeless it seems in the world's eyes. Through prayer and spending time reading the truth of God's word, they draw strength from their heavenly Father, allowing him to make their hearts as strong as they need to be, but as soft as well.

Empowering others

Of course, Compassion was able to help the woman who'd been feeding her twins dog food and make sure new provision was made to take care of that family's needs, but the problem is how you help people over the long term. That's one of the things I love about the work of Compassion, and others like them. They are not in the business of patting people on the head, feeling sorry for them and giving them a hand-out. There was a real sense of them wanting to care for people's physical and spiritual needs and empower them not to be dependent on others. They think about the long term, helping people create a future for themselves and their families. Because what happens most of the time is that poor children grow up to become poor adults who go on to have poor children, and so the cycle continues.

One of the key things Compassion does is secure sponsorship for children, giving them the opportunity to get an education to help break this vicious cycle. Many of us sponsor children because we know it's a good thing to do, but we don't always know the incredible difference it can really make. Sponsoring one child in a country like Bolivia can break the cycle of poverty and change the future of that child, their family and the future generations of their family. It's not about hand-outs; it's about offering others the opportunities that we can take for granted and giving people the best possible chance to make a decent living and a decent life for themselves and their families. In Bolivia only 18 per cent of young people graduate from high school, but if we could change that, what a difference it could make for the future. The work of Compassion highlights the positive cycle we can create if we step in and get involved.

Josue is eighteen years old and lives in the Bolivian town of Cochabamba. His father saw no value in Josue getting an education; he treated him poorly and made his son work with him as a bricklayer from a young age. When Josue got involved with a Compassion project at the age of seven, he said he often went just to get away from home. However, over the years he met with Jesus and has gone on not only to graduate from high school but to start studying civil engineering at university. He hopes to run his own construction business, where he plans to pay his staff to spend half an hour a day reading the Bible, with the hope of helping many in the industry who rely on alcohol like his father does. In addition to his studies, Josue returns to the Compassion centre to help younger children because he says his sponsor inspired him to help others and show them the kindness he himself has received. Doesn't that feel like how life is supposed to be? You see someone in need, you help them; they see someone in need, they help them. That's the kind of cycle we can be a part of creating if we get involved.

One of the other things I love about Compassion is that they understand that you need to take a holistic approach to working with people, not just focusing on education alone. They teach children about hygiene and nutrition (information which is also passed on to their families), they deal with social and emotional issues, they run programmes that help fathers connect with their children where they haven't previously been very involved in their lives. They teach parents income-generating skills so that they have the means to support themselves and their children. Vitally, they look after people's spiritual needs, doing everything they can to introduce the people they work with to Jesus, and helping them develop a strong relationship with him. They bring hope for today and hope for eternity.

It was incredibly encouraging to hear stories of lives being turned around, but the family I had met who had seven children only had sponsorship for two to go to school. I wanted to know what happened to the rest of the family. "We share everything," the children told me. It turns out that the two who go to school teach their brothers and sisters how to read and write so that they all benefit from the education. It's so easy to be overwhelmed by the need when the reality is that every bit of help can make a huge difference and have a positive knock-on effect.

Restoring hope

It's hard to overestimate the impact that bringing hope back to people can have. Charities like Compassion show individuals and families living in poverty that someone cares. Someone cares enough to part with their money in order to sponsor a child they don't know. Someone cares enough to leave their life, get on a plane and go and work in a town or village in a different part of the world to improve the lives of the people there. If you're living in a desperate situation, knowing that someone is concerned for you and someone is committed to helping you change your life can mean a great deal. It can bring you real, tangible, life-changing hope.

Hope is hard to measure but it's vitally important to deliver. We live in a society that is becoming increasingly obsessed with targets; as the CEO of a charity I get asked all the time about how we can measure what we do. Obviously it's absolutely vital to be accountable to the people who support you and sometimes targets and statistics can be really helpful. But sometimes we need to remember that some of the most important things in life can't actually be measured. How can you measure the hope you've reignited in a person, a family or a community? How can you statistically show the increased amount of love someone felt because you got involved in their situation? Richard Stearns, the CEO of World Vision, said:

At World Vision, we often say that "hope" is our most enduring legacy. If we can revive in a community of people their belief in themselves – if we can rekindle their almost extinguished hopes for a better future for their children – then we have accomplished much more than just punching a water well into the ground. This is the art and spirituality of development. The triumph of the human spirit is not easily measured.[1]

Restoring dignity

When we look at how Jesus responded to people in poverty, we learn a huge amount about the approach we should take. In Jesus' day, people believed that if you were poor you deserved to be, so they were given no status or dignity and were excluded from life. I just love reading the gospel accounts of how Jesus treated people who society said were nothing, giving them special honour and privilege, much to everyone's amazement. One such story that I find remarkable is when Jesus encounters Bartimaeus.

Bartimaeus was an outcast because he was blind. He was seen as undesirable, cursed by God. He spent his days sitting by the roadside begging for money. His family had probably disowned him, as that happened frequently to those with disabilities in that culture. Even the disciples thought he wasn't worth bothering with, and wasn't important enough to distract Jesus from what he was doing.

As Jesus passed, Bartimaeus shouted out, "Jesus, Son of David, have mercy on me" (Mark 10:47). He couldn't see physically but spiritually he could see that Jesus was the one who would reign on David's throne, as the prophecies had said. He could see more clearly, therefore, than most of Jesus' disciples. When they tried to stop him, he just shouted all the louder – his desperation obvious, his belief that Jesus could do something for him making him unafraid of the crowd.

Jesus stopped in his tracks and called Bartimaeus to him, asking, "What do you want me to do for you?" Jesus wasn't playing dumb. By asking this question he was doing for this man's soul what his physical healing would do for his body. Here we see how the Messiah, the great longed-for Saviour, the greatest man who ever lived, interacted with a man cast out by society and possibly rejected even by his own family. He stopped what he was doing and offered to serve him. He gave the man dignity by giving him a choice and by paying him attention. He paused to make sure Bartimaeus knew he was worth so much more than he'd ever been told. Imagine how the crowd, who had been telling him to shut up, felt when they saw just how much Jesus cared for him. He gave him his sight, his faith in himself, his place in society and his place in the kingdom of heaven. Bartimaeus, who had spent his days wrapped in the only security he had – a cloak – threw that cloak aside, jumped to his feet and followed Jesus. Having encountered such love and respect, it's no surprise that Bartimaeus dropped all the security he'd ever known and followed this man who had given him back his life in more ways than one.

"Them and us"

Jesus didn't divide society up into rich and poor. He didn't give special honour to those the world honoured; in fact he went to the other extreme to redress the balance.

When I look at the people who do the most amazing work, I realize they don't have a sense of "them and us" because they grasp there is only "us". I am passionate that we, as God's people, should get to grips with this. It transforms the way we look at social action and how we care for the poor. Social action stops being something we think we should do. Instead, it becomes a heart of love that's desperate to help any brother or sister in need. When we think we're two separate groups of people we can easily be condescending; when we know we're one, there's nothing patronizing in our actions.

I find myself speaking about Mother Teresa all the time, because she seems to be one of the people who have best embodied this kind of thinking in the last hundred years. Because of her work, 500,000 families were fed every year, 90,000 people with leprosy were loved and looked after, and 27,000 friendless people died with a dignity that would otherwise have been lacking.

Her dangerous story is about so much more than that, though. What Mother Teresa understood is that charity is not *condescending* but *ascending*. She knew that in serving the poor and the weak, she was in fact serving Jesus whom she loved more than anything else. Her example continues to amaze us, many years after her death, because she truly loved. She loved with everything she had and it changed the world and inspired millions of people.

I find it interesting that she didn't keep caring for people because she knew God's presence or heard him continually telling her to. Her journals make for quite hard reading when it comes to her relationship with God. You'd imagine someone like Mother Teresa would have a twenty-four-hour hotline to Jesus, hearing his voice and knowing his encouragement at every turn. The reality was that she went through some really dark times when she felt totally isolated and alone, so we know her actions weren't based on her feelings. She was obedient to serving those in need, no matter what it cost her. It can give us courage, because she too had her doubts. She wasn't superhuman but she was inspired by love. She was amazing and deserves the praise she gets, but ultimately she was just a human being trying to reflect the love of her heavenly Father.

When we are motivated by love we stop seeing people as mission projects or people we are helping. They become friends, people we care about, people whose lives we are involved in. That is what I want for the people XLP works with and it is my hope that as God's church we will grasp the same thing, because part of being a Christian is getting to grips with the fact that these people, who are starving and have so little money that they need to feed their babies dog food, are our brothers and sisters. As Desmond Tutu said:

> *Would you let your brother's or sister's family, your relatives, eke out a miserable existence in poverty? Would you let them go hungry? And yet every 3.6 seconds someone dies of hunger and three-quarters of these children are under five. If we realized that we are family, we would not let this happen to our brothers and sisters.*[2]

When we lose our "them and us" mentality we realize we have a lot to learn from others. We realize our friends can teach us just as much as we can teach them. We discover the privilege of praying for them and having them pray for us. We see some of the richness of other cultures and things we can learn from a different way of life. Often we find that where there is a lack of material wealth, there is an abundance of love and a genuine community – something we need to rediscover in our over-indulged but often lonely society.

Chapter 3

Hope for Young People

I started the charity XLP after there was a stabbing in a school near to the church where I was a youth worker.

The school invited me to come and speak to them, and I started to realize how different life was for these kids from how it had been for me growing up. Many of us find our teenage years hard to navigate, with all their predictable pressures and problems as we try to leave behind our youth and grow into young adults. For many young people today, life seems to have additional pressures. Bullying is increasing, teenage depression and anxiety are prolific, the average age of people becoming sexually active is decreasing, gangs are on the rise, and violence amongst teenagers is at an all-time high. Many are struggling to deal with the breakdown of their family unit, getting a place at university is harder and harder and, added to all of this, degree or not, they're constantly told there aren't enough jobs for them and they're likely to spend a good deal of time unemployed. Life is tough and the outlook can be bleak.

Despite all of this, the young people we work with week in, week out show amazing resilience and courage in the face of many obstacles. Many of them have been written off by their schools or families but we want to show them that someone cares, someone believes in them. Often the situations they face seem hopeless and they can't see a way out for themselves, so we want to see for them with the eyes of hope.

One of the frustrations I hear from young people all the time is that they feel as though no one listens to them. No one likes to be ignored. It is incredibly frustrating, it alienates people, and inevitably it leads to a breakdown in relationship. It is important that when we've got something to say, others listen – but young people often feel that their voice just isn't heard. They can find it hard to articulate all the complex issues of their lives, especially when they are dealing with issues like family breakdown, financial and emotional poverty, poor housing, educational failure, gangs and drugs, fear and hopelessness. Sometimes they just can't find anyone who will listen and understand how difficult life is for them.

At XLP, we wanted to do something to change that for the young people we work with, and we hit upon the idea of putting on Arts Showcases. We run a competition through schools and all the pupils are invited to act, dance, sing or rap about the issues in their life and community. We then put on a show of the best acts who perform in front of friends and family and compete to be the overall Showcase winner. It's amazing to see the parents of kids who are often in trouble suddenly realizing the talent that their son or daughter has and experiencing a new pride in their child. At our most recent showcase, after I had announced the results, the parents of two of the winners left their seats at the back of the theatre, jumped onto the stage and hugged their kids and me (to the amusement of the audience). They were actually crying because they were so overwhelmed that their kids had won. For me, the best thing about it is giving each young person the chance to have their say, and the fact that it gives us an opportunity to build a relationship with young people and their families.

Relationship is foundational to the kingdom of God. If we want to develop strong relationships with young people, we need to listen to them, not allowing preconceived ideas to make us judgmental, and it will require courage and commitment. These are true values of the kingdom of God that bring hope to young people and are key to enabling us to engage whilst maintaining our Christian distinctive.

Over the years I have been blown away by the acts in our showcases. Sometimes there are brilliant, high-energy performances while the young people show off their dancing skills. Other times you'll be moved to tears by a song that speaks of the pain in someone's life. Often when you're talking to a young person they'll say things like: "You've no idea what I've seen or what I've been through." The Showcase gives them a chance to tell everyone. Joe, from a school in East London, performed this:

> *You can call me a child of war*
> *But I bet you haven't seen half the stuff that I*
> *   saw*
> *There's always fighting out on the streets*
> *Battles break out between thugs and police*
> *At the moment the crime rate is so high*
> *If we don't do something about it now more people*
> *   will die*
> *But it's hard not to fall into that kind of life*
> *When you're surrounded by drugs, guns and*
> *   knives.[1]*

I asked Joe about the lyrics and he said he wrote them after a friend was stabbed. He said, "It's about the things I've seen and experienced on the streets. It's about young people ending up getting involved in bad stuff. I'm not excusing it; I'm just telling it how it is. I want people to hear my music to realize that what they are doing is wrong." Instead of taking out his anger on the people who stabbed his friend, he was able to communicate his feelings through music.

Another act that will always stand out in my mind was

when two girls – Rachel and Sharlene – put on a sketch. The audience was a volatile one with kids from different postcodes, who are normally fighting with each other, sitting in the same room. Just months earlier, the community had been devastated by the murder of an innocent fifteen-year-old boy, Michael Dosunmu. Two men had burst into Michael's house in search of his older brother, who they believed owed them money. In a case of mistaken identity they shot Michael, a church-going schoolboy, as he slept in his bed. This is what Rachel and Sharlene said as part of their Showcase piece:

Have you any idea what it's like to walk into your brother's bedroom and see him swimming in a pool of his own blood? Do you have any idea how it feels to walk in and see him struggle for one breath? Do you have any idea how it feels to watch your brother suffocate on his own collar-bone because some idiot ran into our house and shot him? My little brother who was gonna grow up and look after us – gone. For what? SE15, SW9. What's that? A couple of numbers? A couple of letters of the alphabet?

We the youth – each one of us – has the potential to grow up and change this world. So if you're telling me that "us" – the future aro stabbing each other and going in each other's houses and shooting each other, taking lives like we can give them back – tell me this – what kind of future are we gonna be?

You could have heard a pin drop as the power of their words hit home around the auditorium. It was an incredibly poignant moment as these girls, who had lost a friend, challenged their peers to think about the consequences of their actions. If I had stood up and said exactly the same words, the kids would probably have said, "OK, Patrick. Whatever!" Yet a fifteen-year-old girl, who stands up in front of her own community and says that, has a power I could never have. Hearing the truth from people living with the pain of losing loved ones made all the difference.

A God of mercy and grace

Two of our biggest barriers to sharing the hope of the kingdom of God are, firstly, that we often share "the truth" as we see it rather than as Jesus sees it, and secondly, that we share truth without love. If we do this we can appear, and are, very judgmental.

"Do not judge" is one of the simplest commands in the whole Bible and arguably one of the hardest to keep. We can't seem to stop ourselves from jumping to conclusions and buying into stereotypes. We let the world inform our perceptions of people rather than Jesus. We do it without even realizing it and we make damaging judgmental decisions about people in the blink of an eye. I remember once shouting at a kid who was talking through a class I was giving at a school in London. I thought he was being "like all kids of that sort" – disruptive and disrespectful. He quietly responded by telling me that he was translating what I was saying for the boy next to him, who didn't speak English. I felt awful!

Carly, one of XLP's youth workers, runs an after-school club on a London estate where she gathers a big group of kids to have dinner together. From day one it was an absolute nightmare: the kids would be on their mobiles the whole time, getting up and down from the table, arguing and shouting. One day the frustration got too much and Carly yelled at them, "How many of you behave like this when you eat at home?" As she looked around, all she saw were blank faces looking back at her and understanding slowly dawned. "How many of you have family meal times?" she asked. Not a single hand went up. Not one of those young people had ever sat down to a family meal. They had no concept of how to behave at the meal table because no one had ever told them. They ate in their bedrooms, in front of the TV, or grabbed something on the go.

Suddenly Carly's perception changed from seeing a bunch of disrespectful and rude kids, to seeing young people who had never experienced the pleasure of eating together as a family, because of the chaos of their home life. She realized that what they needed was someone to teach them about what it means to eat together and be family. Calming them down, she laid some basic ground rules: no phones, no farting and no leaving the table without asking! She encouraged them to talk to each other, find out about each other, and discuss different topics whilst they ate together.

These kids have changed now. They hold real conversations, they share their successes and struggles with each other, they eat together and they are developing a new understanding of being family. We have to learn to look past people's behaviours and to listen to and understand them; only then can we offer hope of a different future.

Letting the kingdom of God inform our perception and understanding of young people will mean being radical. It requires courage and commitment to go against the negative stereotyping that is so prevalent in the media. The newspapers build a picture that young people are violent, out-of-control, wild, crazy, drug-addicted, drunk, knife-wielding thugs who have no regard for their families or others in society. The media insinuate that they don't care about school or employment and are basically hell-bent on self-destruction. As the urban riots in the UK in 2011 played out on our TVs we were all shocked at the scenes of violence, destruction and looting that were taking place. Instantly all young people living in our inner cities seemed branded by the press as violent gang members and deserving of severe treatment by police and the justice system.

I wrote in a number of national newspapers at the time that we urgently need to remember that those involved in these deplorable acts do not represent the vast majority of teenagers and young people who live in our communities. I know many young people who were appalled and saddened by what was happening, got involved in helping to clear up and publicly condemned the actions of their peers. Maybe we know in our hearts the media don't give us a true representation, but how do you react if you see a group of young people hanging around on a street corner? It's all too easy to buy into the stereotypes and feel scared and nervous just because they are teenagers.

Recently, a councillor in Wales called for all teenagers in the area to be given a 9 p.m. curfew to try and stem the number of young people being arrested. His intention (aside from getting a newspaper headline) was probably good, but what he succeeded in doing was alienating a lot of young people who had done nothing wrong and were rightly angry at being treated like criminals because of other people's behaviour.

We have to be really wary of stereotypes and get to know the real person we are trying to work with. When we get to know individuals we start to see that even if some of their outward behaviour does match up to the stereotypes, there will undoubtedly be reasons as to why, and what they need is help, not simply to be written off. When society responds negatively to people, it turns them into outcasts – from their schools, their communities, and even their families. They find themselves frustratingly excluded from mainstream society, but the good news is that even those who have become such outcasts have a place in God's kingdom! I truly believe there is hope for our young people, but others often look at the media headlines and ask me why I have that hope.

For me, the key is seeing past who they are now and seeing what they have the potential to become. They are no different to any of us; they have just been born into a different situation and have not had the same chances we've had. We must remember that gang members are not born as criminals but as children, who grow into young people trapped in a cycle of hopelessness generated by issues including family breakdown, poor housing, financial, emotional and aspirational poverty, educational failure and youth unemployment. I'm all too aware that if I had been born into a different family, had a different upbringing or gone to a different school, my life could have looked just like theirs.

A God of truth, courage and commitment

If we really want to give hope to young people, then we will need courage and commitment, firmly rooted in trusting Jesus with our own lives. We sometimes worry that by accepting and loving people as they are we will be, or will be seen to be, condoning their actions. Perhaps we are even worried what other people might say about us if we are discovered engaging with the "wrong" people.

However, Jesus radically put his concern for those who

were lost and need his hope of the kingdom message before concern for his own reputation or well-being. He understood that what people need to be offered if they are to change their life, is a radical new type of relationship where mercy and grace go hand in hand with uncompromising truth, courage and commitment. Only a relationship like this can turn people's lives upside down and transform their future life and even their eternity.

One of the most famous examples of this is Jesus' encounter with Zacchaeus (Luke 19:2ff), who was a traitor in the eyes of the Jewish people. He was not only collecting money for the Roman overlords from a population who were mostly already extremely poor, but he was also skimming even more money off for himself. He was despised and considered so unholy that he wouldn't have been allowed to come near to God by entering the Temple.

To eat with someone in first-century Israel was an incredibly intimate affair. It was something you did with very close friends and family, so no true Israelite would have considered eating with such a sinner as Zacchaeus. However, in the face of criticism and at risk to himself, Jesus took the initiative and invited himself to dinner with Zacchaeus. For Jesus, no one is irredeemable or outside of the scope of his interest and love, not even Zacchaeus. Jesus could see something that others could not; he could see past what Zacchaeus had done and become, and he saw who he could become. He didn't tell Zacchaeus that everything he was doing was OK, but he showed Zacchaeus that he still loved him anyway.

When he was confronted with the truth and the love of God in a way that cost the giver, Zacchaeus could, perhaps for the first time, see the reality of who he had become and all the possibilities of what he could be instead. That's the first step to hope: realizing that you need help and that it is being offered to you. The second step is that it needs to be acted upon. Zacchaeus responded to the hope of the good news of the kingdom of God and chose to embrace his newfound future right there and then. He committed to repaying all he'd taken and making generous amends for what he had done.

Time and again Jesus refused to let his understanding of God's kingdom be defined or limited by the customs and assumptions of the day; for Jesus, everyone was welcome and it was the kingdom of God that needed to inform the behaviours and attitudes of the people rather than the other way around. What Jesus did and said revealed the true nature of the hope that is found in the kingdom of the living God. He engaged in conversation and ate meals with all the "wrong" people – they were the wrong age, the wrong sex, the wrong ethnicity, had the wrong jobs, the wrong illnesses and had done all the wrong things – definitely not, according to the wisdom of the day, candidates for membership in God's kingdom. He chatted to the Samaritan woman in a culture where women were of little value and Samaritans were hated. He embraced children in a world where they had no worth. He actively sought out and spent time with the sick, prostitutes, tax collectors and even senior-ranking officials and soldiers from the overlord nation who occupied Israel. Yet he did more than just fraternize with these rejects from first-century Jewish society; he held up their response to the offer of the kingdom of God as an example! He earned himself the name "Friend of Sinners". It's a title we don't think too much about today but it offers us an incredible insight into the true heart of a loving God.

Wouldn't it be amazing if we could offer God's truth alongside God's love in this way? How different would our young people look if we had the eyes of Jesus? That should be our daily prayer – that we would see past what people have become and see what they could be.

Working *with* young people

Part of this process is getting to know people. One of the things we emphasize at XLP is that we want to find solutions to problems in a community by working *with* that community, not by doing things *for* them or *to* them. If we want to be a blessing to young people, the last thing we want to do is make assumptions about them, parachute into their lives and patronize them by thinking we already have all the answers. We can have great intentions and mean well, but if we don't get involved and really understand their lives (for good and bad), we're unlikely to bring any long-term solutions. As believers it is absolutely key that we are engaged with and serving the poor and the marginalized outside of the church, and to do that effectively we need to get to know them and offer them a place right at the heart of the life of our church community. Jesus found those who were considered to be outside of God's kingdom and offered them a place right at the heart of it.

One of the most important things to a young person is to have an accessible role model in their lives: someone who will listen to them, take them seriously, hear their concerns, help them to make wise choices, and help them to discover a sense of hope for the future and to realize their God-given potential. For many young people, the sad reality is that they have no such role model to set an example for them, to help them and to work *with* them.

We started a mentoring project at XLP called XL-Mentoring. It works with some of our most at-risk young people who are on the verge of exclusion or have already been excluded, and/or are at high risk of involvement or are already involved in gangs. We recruit and train volunteer mentors drawn from local churches who agree to spend around two hours with their young person each week and keep up with them in between through texts. It's a simple idea that could work anywhere, but it's had astonishing results. Of the first twenty kids we took into the project, after twelve months eighteen of them were still in mainstream education and 90 per cent, as far as we know, refrained from criminal or antisocial behaviour (the other 10 per cent were relatively minor incidents!). Of course, the relationship between the mentor and the young person is not always easy, particularly in the early days, and requires great patience, perseverance and understanding by the mentor, but once a trusted relationship is established, true and lasting change is possible.

We know of examples where young people are born on an estate and told by the adults in their lives that they will never amount to anything, that they will grow up, live, and eventually die, still living on that estate. Little encouragement is offered and in the end they believe what they are told and any hope they had for the future quickly dissolves. Our mentors help these young people to rediscover who they really are and the incredible potential they have. The key to change comes when a young person believes they have a place in the world and that there is a purpose and a meaning to their lives. It is this that the mentor helps them to find, and when they do, unbelievable changes can take place.

One fantastic example is Sarah. She was referred to us because her school was concerned about her isolation and apparent lack of boundaries, especially with boys and men. She was living with her aunt's family and there was a history of child protection issues. Her school were worried she would be targeted by a gang and she was on the verge of exclusion from school. Sarah was keen to join XL-Mentoring because she desperately wanted a trustworthy adult who would listen to her; she said that she usually had to keep how she really felt a secret. Sarah met with her mentor and began to open up to her, tackling some of the issues that were going on in her life together. The school began to see a big improvement in Sarah's behaviour, so much so that after nine months she had gone from nearly being excluded to being nominated for Head Girl by her teachers! That's real transformation, and she is now being held up as a positive example to her peers.

A God of real hope, not fantasy

Although the XL-Mentoring programme is very simple in principle, it's not ever straightforward. People are messy, illogical and unpredictable, and often don't do what is in their own best interests. If all we do is tell our success stories, we're not giving anyone the full picture and there's a very real danger in us only telling tales of things working out well – we'd be living in a fantasy world. Jesus always dealt with the gritty reality of the world he inhabited and didn't shy away from the fact that life isn't always smooth or easy. So whilst we have many stories like Sarah's, where we've seen astonishing transformation, we also have many stories of times when we've thought a young person was doing really well and then we've had a phone call to say they've gone to prison, got pregnant, been kicked out of home or school, been caught with drugs or even been killed.

You can imagine how devastating it is to hear those things if you've truly got to know the young person involved and can count them as a friend, or even family. I have sat in meetings as XLP staff have cried and grieved over the loss of a young person they have worked with over many years. The truth is, there are no quick fixes for people's lives and things often look very messy for a long time. Working with young people is a rollercoaster; things go up but they also plummet back down. We can't go into any kind of youth work with an agenda of making everything nice and neat – if we do, we'll be disappointed. Youth workers and mentors have to be courageous and committed, offer grace and mercy and be people who listen and share in the lives of others.

You have to be committed for the long haul. There is no room for any Hollywood notion that you can take someone from complicated and difficult circumstances and transform their lives in the time it takes for a feel-good track to play in the background. People just don't work like that. It's a case of working day in, day out with someone, helping them inch forward, encouraging them when they've slipped back and being there for them, come what may. Sometimes it has incredible rewards, other times it feels like a long, hard slog. If we go into youth work with our hopes based on a fantasy of change coming easily, we'll be disappointed and tempted to give up at the first hurdle because we think we're doing something wrong. Young people need to be invested in. We mustn't swoop in hoping for a quick fix; we need to be committed to seeing change over a long and often slow process.

Having hope for people doesn't mean being unrealistic. It means we see what is possible but we don't kid ourselves that it will always come easily. But, when change does come, and when it's been worked at and when breakthrough happens, it's like no other feeling on earth, and, in the final analysis, it's worth it. Why? Because you are able to know that in the power of the Holy Spirit you are changing the future of a person – you are taking "people of hopelessness" and restoring them; offering them a place in the kingdom of God for all of eternity.

Chapter 4

Hope for Gangs

Hopeful kids don't join gangs.

Father G, founder of Homeboys

Gangs were a problem I encountered right on my own doorstep. We'd been seeing an increase in knife and gun incidents in the schools we were working in and the media were starting to make noises about gangs becoming rife. It really hit home to me when my daughter (who was seven months old at the time) was awoken by the sound of gunshots just down the road from our London home.

It wasn't just London either. Friends of mine were performing at a gig in Birmingham when two young women were shot dead nearby. Rival gangs were targeting each other and the girls got caught in the crossfire, paying the ultimate price. Over the following months the problems seemed to intensify and so did a sense of unease. More tragic teenage deaths started to make headline news for days at a time, but I soon realized that even they weren't giving us the full picture. Through our work in schools we were often told of people being killed through gang violence; the stories had become so commonplace that they didn't even always make a big splash in the local news.

Another wake-up call for me about how serious this issue was for young people was when I met fifteen-year-old Rakeem, who wore a bullet-proof vest to school. At first I thought it was bravado – why would any teenager in London need a bullet-proof vest? Then I found out that a rival gang, who had already put Rakeem's brother in hospital and shot his cousin, wanted to kill him. Six weeks later Rakeem was stabbed in broad daylight outside his school and narrowly escaped with his life.

Over the years we have seen the violence continue to escalate. We started to see the increase of postcode wars where kids from one area wouldn't go into another postcode which was controlled by a rival gang. Warring gangs would maim each other, even take each other's lives, sparking retaliation attacks that could go backwards and forwards between gangs for years. Gangs seemed to be getting increasingly violent, with fights erupting over nothing and the death toll of teenagers steadily rising. There is nothing more devastating in our work than attending the funeral of a young person who has died through gang violence. One of the hardest things I've ever had to do is look into the eyes of a parent who has lost their child and try to find something, *anything*, to say to offer comfort in the face of such an utterly senseless tragedy. It hits you in the gut that kids are killing each other, leaving a trail of sheer devastation in their wake.

As this violence increased I remember a vicar saying to me, "Who would want to live in Peckham?" At the time I had just moved into the heart of the area. I always knew that the area had a bad reputation, to the extent that many people had questioned whether I really wanted to work and bring my family up there. It's true that it's an area that's had a lot of problems over the years, from high unemployment and rioting in the eighties through to high youth crime and growing gang problems in the new millennium. Yet God had shared something of his love for the people of Peckham with me, and so I was desperate to see it turned round. The same story kept coming back to me from the book of Joshua, where Achan is found guilty of theft and is taken to the Valley of Achor to be stoned (Joshua 7). Achor means "a place of trouble", but later, through the prophet Hosea, God promises he will "make the Valley of Achor a door of hope" (Hosea 2:15). Isn't that the kingdom – taking a place labelled as no good and turning it into a place of hope? I hold on to that for Peckham and many of the similar places where XLP now works, knowing that it's God's heart to change places of violence and despair into places where people's lives are full of purpose and hope. I also felt keenly aware that though neighbourhoods like Peckham have their challenges, we need to be careful about giving them blanket labels. Within these areas are some of the most inspirational people you will ever encounter; people who are meeting the challenges of their area head-on every day.

Perspective

As the gang violence grew I knew that we had to do something to help young people in gangs and at risk of getting into gangs.

The best starting point seemed to be to try and understand the world from their perspective. I just couldn't comprehend what would make someone want to live that kind of lifestyle. Why would you want to put your life in danger and live constantly looking over your shoulder, fearing retaliation? What would make you so full of anger that you could put a knife in someone's chest or shoot them dead?

While I was asking these questions I was approached by the Centre for Social Justice (CSJ), which is an independent think-tank looking for solutions to issues around poverty in the UK. They asked if I would get involved in some research they were doing into gangs and, with some trepidation, I said yes. I was worried, as I'm not very academic and wondered whether I would be able to contribute anything of value to the work of a think-tank. However, it was a fantastic opportunity to understand the situation from a wider perspective and really get to the heart of what was happening.

It seemed that all across the country there was growing fear of gangs but little information around why they were becoming more prevalent. The more we spoke to people, the more we realized there were three worrying developments in the UK gang culture. Firstly, the age that people get involved in gangs has gone down and now kids as young as eight or nine are becoming involved. Secondly, girls are increasingly becoming part of gangs and becoming more violent themselves. Thirdly, the level of violence is rising, with people within gangs trying to outdo each other in terms of who can be the most violent and do the worst thing.

However, we wanted our research to do more than see what was happening; we wanted to discover *why* young people chose to join gangs in the first place. We found a number of key drivers, but it's vitally important to bear in mind that it is rarely one of these factors working in isolation; usually a number will be combined before someone turns to a gang. It seemed persistent poverty, a lack of male role models, educational failure, unemployment, fear, and anger were all playing their part in driving people towards gangs. Many of these drivers perpetuate each other. For example, persistent poverty can make you angry, especially when you grow up in a city where deprivation exists in such close proximity to wealth and prosperity. Often people living from hand to mouth in sky-high concrete tower blocks live only a road away from the plush six-bedroom homes of the wealthy.

The breakdown of the traditional family unit seems to play

are angry about the hand that life has dealt them, angry that they can't make their voice heard, angry because they have seen their dad beat up their mum and they feel powerless to do anything about it, angry that they've lost their friends to knife and gun crime, angry that they've got no money, angry that they've got no prospects, angry that no one seems to care about them and angry that they can't see any future for themselves. They are ready to explode at the slightest provocation, meaning lives are lost over tiny, ridiculous disagreements. Often for kids caught in this cycle, their behaviours and attitudes alienate them from their own families and communities. Many end up excluded from school and embrace the twisted and distorted sense of family offered through gangs, becoming outcasts from society.

So you can see that when a number of these issues are combined, such as family breakdown, poor housing, lack of education, unemployment and the problems of drugs and crime in their neighbourhood, many children and young people can find themselves feeling unloved, unwanted, and with no sense of belonging or hope for the future. One person summarized all these reasons by saying, "Hopeful kids don't join gangs." Kids who feel secure, who have a stable family life, good role models, and a hope for their future, are unlikely to be attracted to being part of a gang. Jules Pipe, Mayor of Hackney, said, "It's extraordinary, the narrowness of vision that some young people have. People living in Hackney who have never been to the West End, let alone further afield... And that probably is a huge issue behind what is driving [involvement in gangs]... poverty of aspiration. That's actually far more a factor in this than alcohol or drugs."[3]

To experience poverty of aspiration is to have no hope for the future. Many of our young people are living with this sense of utter hopelessness. It is one of the most insidious and harmful conditions for any human being; it leaves you with a distorted view of what is right and wrong, and a cynicism and despair that causes you to feel valueless and unable to access community. If we do not give them hope about the positive things they can achieve with their lives, they will embrace the things that will eventually destroy them and all those around them.

LA

As part of the CSJ research, the research team visited Los Angeles. We knew the gang situation in parts of America was already far more developed than ours, so we set off to California to meet with gang experts to see what we could learn from them. Los Angeles is known as the gang capital of the world, and as we met with the LAPD we quickly found out how much further the violence had spread there. It's always hard to get exact figures on how many people are in gangs, but police say they know that some areas have over five active gangs for every square mile. That's as many as sixty-eight gangs in just one town. Some notorious gangs like The Crips have around 13,000 members just in LA, as well as associated gangs elsewhere in California and even further afield.

We thought the school situation was bad in London until we went to a school in LA where there are four different exits for pupils, and you leave according to which gang you're a part of. Imprisoning gang leaders doesn't seem to help, as they are just as powerful when behind bars as they are walking free. The police said there is a shooting every day and they think at least every other one is gang-related. We were shown graphic, stomach-turning images, like a video of a four-year-old girl who was caught in the cross-fire of a drive-by shooting and killed. Everything in me wanted to turn away from the images; all I could think about was how I would feel if anything happened to one of my kids.

It was horrific to see how entrenched and systemic the violence is and how desperate the situation has become. To make matters worse, the police kept saying that the UK would be facing the same situation as LA if we didn't do something now to stop the escalation of gangs.

Their words were ringing in my ears as I watched the images of UK cities filled with rioters just a few years later. The riots seemed to be an explosion of all the violence and tension that had been building up in the UK. Many of them took place in areas where XLP works; the Lewisham riots were just around the corner from our office and the Peckham ones were right where I live. Although it wasn't just gang members who were involved, many of the reasons why someone would take to the streets to loot a shop, burn a building to the ground or antagonize police officers, are the same as why someone would join a gang. Having done the research into what leads someone towards gang life, my heart was breaking for all the people rioting.

Let me be really clear: I don't believe there is any excuse for their behaviour. No matter how hard life gets, there is no reason to do the things that we saw happen on those dreadful evenings where people lost their lives, their homes and their livelihoods. I don't believe we should make excuses for people and I absolutely agree that people should receive appropriate punishment for any part they played in such criminal activities.

All that said, I also believe we can't just condemn people for their actions without asking why they would do such things in the first place. People were amazed that parents would let their young children be out on the streets during a riot. The sad fact is that the majority of those children are left to their own devices on a daily basis and there was nothing unusual in their parents not knowing where they were those nights. It was sickening to see the displays of anger pouring out of people as they smashed in windows and overturned police cars, but I kept coming back to the fact that children aren't born angry. Some people were inevitably swept up in the excitement and got involved in something they would normally have had nothing to do with, but it seemed as if most of the people had nothing to lose.

Isn't that a frightening thought? That thousands who took to the streets felt there was nothing holding them back, no relationships, no job, no future prospects that they would risk by their actions. It seemed to me as though they'd lost all hope. The best thing that a tragedy like the riots can do is make us more honest about what's really happening and face up to the facts. There are thousands of people who feel excluded and on the margins. We need to be addressing the issues, not writing people off. We can't ignore the warnings of people like the LAPD that we need to do something to stop this from becoming a regular occurrence. We need to learn the lessons from places like LA, which have seen gangs and gang violence become endemic, and stop it from happening here.

Whilst my trip to LA was heavy with these warnings and the reality of the situation there, we were also fortunate enough to meet some people who haven't given up on those that society has written off. Their stories were inspiring and fuelled my desire that we should get involved and bring positive change.

Chapter 5
Breaking the Cycle

The value of an education

As so much of XLP's work takes place in schools, I was eager to meet Erin Gruwell, a teacher from Long Beach, California.

Erin is a white middle-class woman who, in the 1990s, took a job teaching a class that had been deemed completely unreachable. A multitude of different gangs were represented in her classroom, racial tensions were running high and the only thing the pupils felt they had in common was that they hated each other, they hated being in school and they hated their new teacher. It would have been understandable if Erin had quit, as her family and friends said she should, but she stuck it out.

I found myself drawn to Erin's story. When I started working in Peckham with kids of many different ethnic backgrounds, people told me it wouldn't work. I had grown up in white middle-class suburban Chelmsford, where having one child at school from Barbados was as multicultural as things got. People told me it was difficult to break down cultural barriers and that I wouldn't be able to reach the kids because I didn't know anything about them. I couldn't deny that I was way out of my depth. I worked with kids who'd been brought up in the midst of wars in places like Afghanistan, Somalia and

Yugoslavia; some had even been child soldiers. Schools would ask for my opinion on things like how to deal with female circumcision, when I had never even come across it before.

No matter what the differences, though, I knew I couldn't give up on these kids. Just because my life hadn't looked like theirs didn't mean I couldn't find ways to reach out to them. I couldn't pretend I had all the answers, or try to act as if I was something I was not. Anyone who has worked with young people for five minutes will know that you have to be genuine or they will see straight through you.

For me, one of the keys to crossing any divide was to give myself an education on different cultures. Over the course of a number of years I researched black history and made a number of visits to countries like Ghana and to the Caribbean to understand where some of the kids in our classes were coming from.

Erin Gruwell was culturally a million miles from her pupils when she showed up in Long Beach. It was her first job and, wearing high heels and a string of pearls, she walked into a classroom full of gang members. People repeatedly told her the class was full of kids who had no hope of ever graduating and she was wasting her time. But she persevered and wouldn't give up. With tensions so high amongst the pupils, she looked for ways to help the class connect with each other, showing them that their skin tone and their cultures might be different, but they were all facing similar issues. She bought them books to read that they could engage with: *The Diary of Anne Frank* and *Zlata's Diary* (the story of a young girl living in Sarajevo during the Bosnian war). The pupils could relate to these girls, growing up with wars being fought around them, dealing with the feelings of isolation and being trapped. Erin also offered the pupils a chance to tell their own stories. She gave them journals to record whatever was going on in their daily lives, and though the journals weren't being graded, the pupils started to fill them in and pass them to her. Erin read the stories they poured out and heard of fathers using belts to beat their daughters, boys being evicted from their family homes because there wasn't enough money to pay the rent, pupils seeing friends shot dead in gang wars. They told stories of fear, neglect, abuse, violence, anger, divorce, suicide, loss, anorexia and pain. Erin began to see the world from their point of view and it became clear why they struggled to concentrate in school or do any homework outside of the classroom.

As the class opened up and saw that Erin wasn't judging them, they began to feel understood for the first time in their lives. They continued writing and named themselves the Freedom Writers (in reference to the Civil Rights Freedom Riders). Slowly their classroom began to change. It became a place where everyone felt safe and connected – a complete 180-degree shift from when there had been so much fear and hostility in the room. Erin worked with 150 pupils in that first year. Every single one had been written off by everyone else. Under her tutelage, every single one graduated from high school. Some were even the first in their family to go on to higher education.

It was such a privilege to meet with Erin and Maria, one of the pupils in that first class she taught. Maria was a third-generation gang girl who, by the age of five, knew to duck if a car drove past slowly because it was likely to mean someone was about to fire a gun. Before she met Erin she didn't think she would live to see the age of seventeen: she felt like her life didn't matter to anyone. It was crazy to her that a teacher would think she had potential. Erin's confidence in her meant she not only graduated but went on to further education and got involved with setting up the Freedom Writers Foundation to help other kids at risk. Maria herself works for the Foundation, training teachers who are working in classes with at-risk pupils.

The story of how the lives of pupils like Maria were turned around was so remarkable that their diaries were made into a book and their tale was turned into a major film starring Hilary Swank. Their programme is highly respected and Maria – the girl who at fifteen had no hope for her life – has even spoken in Congress. It was incredible to meet her and see the reality of a life completely changed because one person had hope for a class that everyone else had written off. Slightly star-struck, I asked Maria to sign my copy of the Freedom Writers book, and she wrote: "May you always see with the eyes of your heart." Her words took me right back to Jesus and the way he saw not what people had become, but all that they could be. That's what Erin did, and that's what changed that class. Everyone else saw a group of delinquent young people who would never amount to anything; Erin saw a group of bright but troubled pupils who needed someone to care. Convinced of what they could be, Erin was willing to go the extra mile to make it happen. It cost her; it wasn't a nine-to-five job that she could go home and forget at the end of the day. What she did had amazing rewards and consequences she couldn't have imagined, but there is a price to pay if we want to get so involved in people's lives. It's tiring, it's messy, it's difficult and it's often lonely. The good news is – and Erin's class is a living testimony to this – *it can be done*!

Breaking the cycle

It was amazing to meet Erin and hear about the things she has achieved in the classroom, but what about all the people who are no longer in education? Kids who don't have a teacher like

Erin, who don't have any hope for their future outside of a gang – what happens to them?

We heard that in LA lots of the people in gangs today had fathers, and sometimes even grandfathers, who were a part of that gang. They inherited their place like a family business. It's very difficult for someone in that situation to break free from gang life. Who can they turn to when all the people around them are in the same predicament?

Once someone has been to prison, things get even harder. Offenders are released back into the community but no one wants to employ them. The majority dropped out of school and have few marketable skills, so once you add a criminal record, there are very few legitimate job opportunities. This leads many to commit crime to get by, so they end up back in prison. We've seen it here in the UK with worryingly high re-offending rates; around half of the people who leave prison after serving their sentence are re-convicted within a year of release.

Something is clearly very wrong. One of the main issues is that around half of prisoners don't have the necessary skills to do 95 per cent of jobs. Prison can also give you an alternative education – one that tells you how to go deeper into crime. You can get links to other criminals, knowledge of how to break more laws; you can get more angry, get into more fights, and leave no better off than when you went in. Or it can be a chance to be rehabilitated, to look at how you ended up there in the first place. That's one of the reasons God asks us to get involved. God wants to set prisoners free. Not in the sense that we let people run riot and never hold them to account for their actions, but in the sense that he never designed for anyone to commit crimes and have their freedom taken away.

So once people leave prison, how do you break this cycle of re-offending? You put yourself in the middle of it. That's what Father G, a Jesuit priest, did when he started a social enterprise called Homeboys, and we had the privilege of meeting him while we were in LA. His motto is "jobs not jails" and he says, "Building prisons to address crime is a little bit like building graveyards to address AIDS; it's ridiculous."[1]

Homeboys began after Father G spoke to many people deeply entrenched in gangs who desperately wanted to get out of that lifestyle, but couldn't see how they could do it. The premise is simple: provide training and jobs for ex-gang members, offering them a new way of life and a whole new future. Homeboys started with a bakery where people were trained to bake cakes, breads and pastries. This was successful and developed into a café so the produce could be sold, plus further jobs were created running and managing the bakery. As things expanded they widened their net to cater for local events and they even have a range of merchandise which ex-gang members are involved in creating and selling.

The approach is holistic and counselling is available to help the guys deal with some of the horrendous things they have seen and been involved in. Homeboys is the only place in LA to offer free tattoo removal, a service taken up by many who come through the doors. Tattoos are used as a way of identifying which gang you're involved in and ex-members are still seen as targets by rival gangs if their tattoo is in place. Removing them is another way the ex-members can show that they've moved on and are starting a new life.

During our visit I met Fabian, who has been around Homeboys for a few years. He told me that he'd been in a gang since he was very young and had been in and out of prison for sixteen years. "Father G saw in me something no one else could see; I couldn't even see it myself," he told me. Fabian's journey wasn't straightforward. He would get involved at Homeboys and start doing well, but then he'd get back on drugs and end up in rehab, or commit a crime and end up back in jail. Fabian explained how Father G has stuck by him through it all: "Now I'm an artist; I've got a job and I want to make Father G proud. He gives us second, third, fourth chances, because he believes we can make it."

Whilst Homeboys sets clear boundaries for those involved, Father G extends grace and welcomes back anyone who wants to start again and create a new life for themselves. He is not only willing to step in and provide training and employment, he also sticks by people, believing that they can be more than another statistic in gang crime. The grace he shows people really struck a chord with these gang members who were so used to people writing them off. Speaking to ex-gang members in LA, I discovered there was a common thread. The more people I spoke to, the more I heard that a key turning point was knowing that God loved them, was interested in their life and that they are made in his image. Father G was demonstrating God's love and had earned the right to speak into people's lives because he took the time to understand them and meet their needs. When they heard the lengths that God went to in order to be in relationship with them, it gave them hope. When they were told that Jesus came for those who had lost their way, their hearts and lives began to be transformed. When they realized the church was a community ready and willing to welcome them in, it became a safe place where they could grow and change.

There is something incredibly powerful when one person loves another as God loves us. It's a love with integrity that doesn't avoid the hard truths. It's a love that is courageous and committed but costs the lover everything. It's a love that comes with mercy, compassion and grace and just keeps on coming, to the point that it hurts. When it does hurt, the love becomes even deeper, richer and more passionate. It's a love that cares; it listens when no one else does, and it hears. True and lasting change only happens as a response to this kind of love. Only this kind of love can reach into the depths of the tragedy that is so often part of people's lives, and lift them out of the pit into a life worth living and an eternity worth dying for. That's what Jesus shows us in his life, that's what the apostles and countless saints throughout history have grasped.

I used to feel I was doing a really good thing by taking God to different schools and estates in London, but God is already in those places! Our job isn't to take him anywhere; it's to discern what he's doing in any given place and join in with it. It's to display his grace, his love, his mercy, his kindness and bring his hope, and then watch as he transforms people's lives. Meeting Erin and Father G was inspiring. Both got involved in hands-on ways. Both did what they could practically, and we must follow their example here in the UK to keep kids in education, support teachers, schools and parents, find ways to break the cycle of offending and provide training and jobs.

Whilst it was painful hearing the LAPD's warning that the UK is headed towards their volatile situation, and the violence of the UK riots brought home just how close that could be, meeting people who are changing lives gave me hope. It is not a foregone conclusion that the UK will end up like that – *but only if we are willing to get involved.* The increase in gang culture we've seen and the behaviour during the riots tell us the situation is very serious, but we still have reason to believe we can bring positive change. We need to follow the examples of people like Erin and Father G and love individuals, because that is what makes the difference. They showed grace and kindness. They gave second chances. They wouldn't give up. The key thing that seems to bring change is what a young person believes about their place in this world, and whether they can find meaning and purpose. Their self-worth, self-image and hope for their lives will ultimately determine what happens in their future.

Chapter 6

Hope for the Homeless

My very first experience of poverty came when I was sixteen. Seeing the desperate situations many people were facing was like a slap in the face.

I had gone on a mission trip to London where we visited Waterloo Bridge, spending time with some of the 200 homeless people who live there in what is known as Cardboard City. I had led a fairly sheltered existence up to that point, growing up in a nice suburban area, and I was shocked to meet people who lived on the streets. Their reality was something I couldn't comprehend.

Home, to me, was the comfortable house I'd grown up in with my family. Home was a place to be myself, to be comforted when I was upset, to be cared for when I was sick, a place to grow and dream, a place where I was loved and supported, a place where I was safe. I couldn't understand what it would be like to have no family around me and no shelter. It was incomprehensible to live through freezing-cold winters with just a thin blanket, to have no place to wash and get clean, to have no protection from the outside world – whether that be a stray dog wanting to sniff round you in the night or people overdosing on a street corner next to you. It opened my eyes to the reality of life outside of my teenage bubble and it was this experience that broke my heart and made me realize I wanted to do anything I could to help people living in poverty.

I went back to Chelmsford, but my heart was changed. Two years later, when I had finished school, I moved to London and volunteered with a project that took a bus to various parts of the city to meet people who were homeless. We gave them food and clothes but the aim was to be there every week and build relationships with them. I got to know the "regulars" and found out some of their stories about how they ended up on the streets. It blew away my stereotypes of the average homeless person when I found this was an issue that affected people of all ages and backgrounds.

There was one guy who slept on the streets during the week and then returned home to his wife at the weekends. He couldn't afford to stay in London but needed to be there for work, so this seemed like his only choice. There were professional men who'd had breakdowns and were suffering from depression. Men who'd owned their own businesses but had lost family through death and divorce, so they'd turned to alcohol until it took over their life. There were young women who'd been sexually abused as children and had used drugs to numb the pain, their lives spinning out of control until they wound up with nothing. I was told about one guy who was homeless who'd frequently been locked in his room as a child; as an adult he found it easier to sleep out on the streets.

It was heart-breaking to get to know these guys and realize it was just another case of "there but for the grace of God go I". Of course, there are many reasons why someone might find themselves without a home, but a study commissioned by Shelter[1] found the reasons most frequently given are:

- Relationship breakdown: 41 per cent.

- Drug and alcohol problems: 31 per cent and 28 per cent respectively.

- Being asked to leave the family home: 28 per cent.

- Leaving prison: 25 per cent.

- Mental health problems: 19 per cent.

As these statistics imply, there is usually more than one reason indicated and these all go alongside other situations such as being evicted from accommodation and problems with benefits payments. It's easy to judge and make assumptions about people's choices when really we have no idea what they've been through or how terrifying it is to find you have nowhere to call home.

When I started working in schools one of the first things I took an RE lesson on was homelessness. I had a little bit of experience from my volunteering and started doing more research so I would be better informed. I knew that could only teach me so much, though; if I wanted real insight I needed to experience it for myself. Sleeping rough for one night, by choice, and with a home to go back to, is only a minuscule glimpse into what it's really like to live on the streets long term, but I wanted to give it a try.

It was early evening on a cold November night when I headed into central London to sleep rough. Though I had the luxury of wrapping up in many layers before I left home, I quickly discovered it wasn't enough to stop the cold from creeping into my bones. I tried to settle down on a street but soon realized it was too uncomfortable and too noisy to think about getting to sleep. Bored, I began to walk the streets. I walked between the crowds of people out having fun and enjoying London life, feeling utterly isolated and alone. My stomach was already growling and the smell of food from restaurants and takeaways had never been more enticing. A quick look at the prices reminded me that these foods were far beyond what someone living on the streets would hope to afford. It suddenly seemed crazy to watch people drinking away hundreds of pounds in wine bars, when people looking in the windows couldn't even afford a sandwich. I was even more aware of the clashing cultures of rich and poor as I walked past a theatre and saw a group getting into a stretch limousine, heading home in luxury after their night out.

A few hours later I was exhausted. I settled down in front of a bank, trying to find a way to get comfortable. I was ridiculously excited to find a piece of cardboard that could act as a sleeping-mat and protect me from the cold ground. I was foolish if I thought it could provide much comfort, though; despite my sleeping-bag, there was no escaping the cold. By now it was late and people were pouring out of the clubs and bars, noisily making their way to the tube or to a taxi. I tried to close my eyes and block them out but the stream was constant. One even urinated right near me; I couldn't believe it. Couldn't he see I was trying to sleep? Either he hadn't noticed me at all or he didn't think I deserved anything more than to sleep next to a place he chose for a toilet. Others did notice me and I felt myself shrink under their stares. Some looked uneasy, as though they didn't know how to react to me. Others looked with palpable disgust, as if I was the scum of the earth. It was a small glimpse of what many homeless people feel: you don't know me, or anything about my life, so why are you looking at me like that? Why are you judging me when you have no idea who I am or what has happened to me?

A few years ago the BBC did a programme called *Rich, Famous and Homeless*, which came about after a challenge from the Big Issue (a charity working with homeless people in the UK). The programme took five celebrities and challenged them to sleep rough around London for ten days. In their starting interviews the celebrities proffered opinions on homeless people that they were lazy, a drain on society, people who didn't want to pay taxes, and one even said they were "bone idle". They maintained they wouldn't beg on the streets and they wouldn't lose their dignity – words that came back to haunt them as they soon found themselves doing just that, as well as scrounging in bins for left-over scraps of food. They spent most of their days walking around and found they were exhausted. They couldn't get comfortable enough to sleep at night and tiredness soon turned into sleep deprivation. The hunger gnawed away at them. Where they were used to people treating them with respect and sometimes even awe, they suddenly felt worthless. One celebrity encountered another homeless person who became aggressive and pulled a knife, bringing home just how vulnerable you are without a door to shut yourself behind. Some of them spent time sleeping in a hostel but found that experience just as terrifying as being on the streets. A number of people in the hostel were high on drugs, whilst others banged on the celebrities' doors throughout the night. The experience was unnerving and frightening. The street broke their self-esteem, leaving them weepy, fearful, angry and demoralized. All of them desperately wanted to go back home and all of them had the joy of doing just that after ten days of living rough. None, I'm sure, have ever looked at a homeless person in the same way again.

During my trip to Los Angeles I made time to visit Skid Row, an area of the city where around 10,000 people sleep rough every night, giving it the largest concentration of homeless people in the whole of the USA.[2] Some estimate that half of the people living there have mental health issues and I was told it would be too dangerous to walk around because of that. The area has historically housed people on low incomes and always had a large number of rough sleepers, but things have become worse in the last forty years, with many old, unsafe buildings being torn down and no money invested to rebuild them. In the 1980s, as the city recognized the growing population of rough sleepers, temporary shelters (known as flophouses) were built, but they offered no more than a bed for the night. There was no provision of other facilities and therefore no way of people getting out of their situation and finding a more permanent solution.

Skid Row was like nothing I had ever seen before. Tents lined the sides of the road for miles. Some people had made makeshift homes of cardboard, others were sleeping on benches. People pushed their belongings along in supermarket trolleys or sat by the side of the road with nothing to do and nowhere to go. Every now and then you'd see a long, long line of people and realize at the end was someone offering a bowl of soup or a sandwich. As you can imagine, the issues are rife: crime, prostitution, drugs, and alcohol. The picture was so bleak, and it was hard to comprehend that this was all taking place just a few miles away from Hollywood.

I saw many children on the streets and it's almost impossible to imagine what life is like for them growing up somewhere like Skid Row. In America there are 1.5 million homeless children – 290,000 in California alone.[3] How hard must it be to survive in school if you're living on the streets? They are often moved around from place to place, they get teased and bullied at each new school for their clothes, their hygiene and for not having a home.

Sometimes when you see situations like these, it's hard to see hope, hard to see the grass growing through the cracks, but thankfully there are people who are making a difference. One project I learned about, Schools on Wheels, provides mentors and tutors for homeless kids to help them get an education and increase their future prospects. The project began in 1993 when one woman began tutoring homeless kids in a park in Santa Monica. The project has grown and now has hundreds of volunteers who work with homeless children by teaching, mentoring and supporting them and their parents in any way they can. They provide uniforms and school supplies, and have two learning centres, one of which is based right in the heart of Skid Row. I visited that centre and it was fantastic to see this haven for children in the midst of such desperate situations on the streets outside. It was a place where kids were able to be kids, use colouring books, play with toys and even use computers. This project, which began in such a simple way, is providing a ray of hope for kids whose futures would otherwise be bleak.

Isaiah's cry for action

Homelessness is a huge problem, but what can we do? Isaiah 58 makes it really clear what God wants from us in these situations. However, throughout the ages, from the days of Abraham and Moses, through all the kings and the prophets, in Jesus' day and through to today, the people of God forget! It's astounding that we can overlook the clear and direct words of the living God, but we do. So often the word of God has been allowed to gently fade in importance in our lives as we keep hold of the bits we like and feel comfortable with, but we gradually let go of the tougher bits that require perseverance and even suffering on our part. In recent years church congregations have perhaps let go of the words of Isaiah 58 and now it's time for us, as God's people, to rediscover God's sense of balance between what goes on inside the church and what we are called to beyond the walls of the church.

I've had the privilege of speaking at lots of different churches but I've often been asked to speak about Jesus and to avoid speaking about politics or the world, as though the two can be divided. We love categories; we love to be able to classify something, because when we can put it in a box we feel we can understand and control it. We do that so often with people to damaging effect, but we also seem to have a passion for separating the "sacred" and the "secular". It's great that we focus on growing a deeper intimacy with God, but the passage in Isaiah reminds us that knowing and loving God goes hand in hand with knowing and loving others. In our worship of God we cannot emphasize one area that happens to take place in church (our Sunday services) and then ignore what happens outside of the church. It's tantamount to saying, "I love God, but I don't love people!"

When Jesus was asked how someone could get eternal life or enter the kingdom of God, he pointed to the scripture, "'Love the Lord your God with all your heart...' and, 'Love your neighbour as yourself'" (Luke 10:27). When questioned about who this "neighbour" really is, Jesus told the story of the Good Samaritan to illustrate that we are to love *all* people, even our very worst enemy! With that in mind, how can we go on ignoring those outside of the church, particularly the poor and the vulnerable, whilst worshipping so fervently inside church, thinking that it's OK with God?

Isaiah 58 says it isn't OK at all! The passage starts with God's people getting frustrated that God isn't listening to them and asking him why he's not answering their prayers or noticing their fasts. God seems equally frustrated with them. They were focusing on all the stuff inside the church (so, in their own eyes, they were loving God), but they were ignoring people outside of the church. They weren't loving people, caring for the poor and dealing with the injustices all around them. Loving God and loving people are inseparable concepts. To experience the love of God, we need to love people, and to experience the love of people, we need to love God. The people in the time of Isaiah seemed to think that if they did the right things towards God, that would be enough.

If we're honest, don't we sometimes fall into the same trap? We think if we attend church, sing the right songs, read our Bibles, get our kids into a Christian school, and attend a weekly Bible study, we're doing all right. These things are all well and good but they are not the whole picture.

Through Isaiah, God tells us how worthless those actions are on their own if they're not backed up with a lifestyle that reflects God's heart and includes reaching out to people around us. God doesn't leave us guessing what he truly wants; he makes it clear the kind of fast he's after. He wants us to share our food with the poor, give shelter to the homeless and free the oppressed, and not exploit others. He wants the poor and the vulnerable set free from the social structures that keep them in poverty; he wants to do away with systems that make the rich richer and the poor poorer. He calls us to care:

> *What I'm interested in seeing you do is:*
> *sharing your food with the hungry,*
> *inviting the homeless poor into your homes,*
> *putting clothes on the shivering ill-clad...*
> Isaiah 58:7, *The Message*

If we're not careful we can think the only way to find intimacy with God is to do a Bible study. That is definitely not a bad thing, but if it's all we do, we miss the point. The prophets cry out to us to pour ourselves out on behalf of the poor, and tell us in doing so we will find true intimacy with God:

> *"... He defended the cause of the poor and needy,*
> *and so all went well. Is that not what it means to*
> *know me?" declares the Lord.*
> Jeremiah 22:16

We don't need to earn God's favour; we don't serve people to score brownie points. The more we get to know God, the more our hearts should be in line with his, so the things he cares about should become the things we care about. This isn't supposed to be a guilt trip; this is about becoming what God always intended us to be. It's not only the right thing to do, but God tells us it's a prescription for our own well-being too:

> *your healing will quickly appear… The Lord will guide you always; he will satisfy your needs in a sun-scorched land and will strengthen your frame. You will be like a well-watered garden, like a spring whose waters never fail.*

Isaiah 58:8, 11

The words of Isaiah are a cry for action. They speak of hope for the oppressed, hope for the poor, the homeless, the hungry, and hope for those in the church too. Isaiah is telling us to help the homeless person on Skid Row who thinks of themselves as a refugee in their own country; to reach the mothers who prostitute themselves to earn enough money to feed their kids; to bring hope to the children who are homeless and consequently are unlikely to make it through school.

Isaiah asks us to *break* the yoke – not simply to untie it but to break it (verse 6) – so these things can never happen again. Isaiah tells us that God says that if we do this, the lights will turn on and he will answer us when we pray (verses 8–9). This is the hope for the church.

The key to the church receiving from God what it truly desires is to see worship not just as something that happens amongst Christians in the confines of the church building. It's to see the church from God's perspective as something that is truly inclusive and embraces all the passion, compassion, sacrifice, commitment and love of God for the poor, the marginalized, the suffering. That's what "setting the captives free" is all about; at its essence it's about loving people and loving God.

The Bible is more concerned with the issues of poverty and injustice than with so many of the things we get hung up about. If we are serious about following God, these words from Isaiah give us a blueprint to do it. Isaiah 58 inspires me to spend myself on behalf of the poor (verse 10); I'll never quite reach it but I'm always aiming to give more and do more. If we want to lead others to do the same, we need to inspire them too and lead by example. It doesn't work to hit people over the head with guilt; we need to be showing them how to get involved practically and put God's desires into action.

Starting small

We don't always have to start with a ten-year strategy; sometimes starting small makes the most sense.

I love the story of how a charity that works with homeless people, Watford New Hope Trust, started when one woman became a Christian and took literally these words from Isaiah. Janet, along with a friend, began to invite guys who were homeless into her home for a meal each week. The men were not only given a good meal, but had an opportunity to sit at a dinner table and have some dignity restored to them that is all too elusive for someone living on the streets. As Janet got to know the guys, she began to understand what their lives were like and began to see other opportunities to help them. What began with such a simple step has grown over the last fifteen years into a well-respected charity that offers a day centre, a night shelter, supported accommodation, social-enterprise opportunities and much, much more. All because Janet took to heart God's word and put it into practice.

A friend of mine runs a Salvation Army church in London. The church community really wanted to provide a safe place for anyone who is homeless, somewhere relationships could be built and people could be supported. They started by providing healthy food to make sure people got something decent to eat, but decided not to run a regular drop-in session. They felt the temptation was for people to come by for food but hide behind a newspaper, giving them little opportunity to get to know them. They decided to run courses instead called AWAKEN to get people to engage with their skills and gifts and find ways for them to develop in those areas. They run courses on cookery, photography and computer skills, take day trips to museums and spend time making cards. They run a discipleship lunch alongside it where anyone can come and chat about Jesus, plus they have a prayer surgery where leaders of the church are always available to chat and pray. What a fantastic way to demonstrate God's love in word and deed.

Another church I know got involved in a Robes project where churches can open their doors for people who are homeless to sleep inside during the coldest months of the year. They have dinner together, watch a film and then the guys all just want to get to bed, grateful to have somewhere safe to sleep for the night. My friend said it's one of the most powerful worship experiences, seeing thirteen homeless guys asleep at the foot of the cross in his church.

Offering a shelter for the night, which in the winter months can literally make all the difference between life and death, has meant the church has got to know the guys and good relationships have formed. Again, it was from this place that they were able to see further opportunities to help. Sometimes small practical things, like helping someone apply for a job or giving them a place to get cleaned up ahead of an interview, can make all the difference and help someone turn their life around.

You don't even have to start your own project; many towns and cities already have organizations that work with homeless people and most would love the help of additional volunteers. Helping out could mean anything from serving tea and coffee in a day centre to donating clothes. One woman I know of knits hats for people who are homeless every winter and donates them to her local homeless charity. Another youth group, who are perhaps too young to work directly with people who are homeless, meets on a Sunday to make sandwiches that are given to the local homeless day centre for use on the Monday. There are plenty of opportunities to serve!

It's absolutely vital to offer food to someone who is starving. Not only is it biblical, it's common decency. But giving someone a bowl of soup doesn't offer them any hope beyond that meal. It's when we get involved in people's lives and support them in other ways that we can help them find a future away from the streets, and hopefully help them turn things around. You will rarely find a homeless person in London who doesn't know where they can get food, but you will find many who live without hope, believing they will never amount to anything.

A friend of mine, Emily, has worked with people who are homeless for many years and she's told me amazing stories of how the charity she works for has helped countless people turn their lives around. People like George, who was a social worker who worked with homeless and vulnerable young people until his parents became critically ill and he had to move to Jamaica to look after them. When he returned to the UK he found he'd been evicted from his council flat because he'd let someone else stay there while he was gone. He was too proud to ask anyone for help so he started sleeping on the streets. Eventually he got in touch with a local Christian charity that runs a day centre for homeless people. They helped him get into a hostel and access benefits; they talked with him and prayed with him and supported him back into renting his own flat and working part time.

Adam became homeless at the age of thirty-two when his partner of seventeen years asked him to move out of the family home. Heartbroken at losing his wife and two children, he went to stay with a friend. That friend offered him drugs to help ease the pain and Adam quickly became addicted to heroin. He lost his job and started to commit crimes to pay for his addiction, spending eight years in and out of prison, sleeping rough or staying in hostels. At the day centre he spent time chatting to a retired vicar who offered to pray with him. Adam said he felt the love of God come out of the vicar and flow throughout his whole body. He felt as if he was floating two feet above the ground. He gave his life to Jesus, started going along to church and gave up both crime and drugs. The day centre helped him get a flat and get back in contact with his children.

But Emily is quick to point out that "success" is hard to measure and it's rare that everything is solved immediately. Though Adam's life now looks completely different to when he lived on the streets, things can still sometimes be painful in the same way that life can be painful for all of us. At crisis points it's a daily choice for people like Adam who are recovering from addictions not to turn back to old coping mechanisms. When Adam's mother recently passed away, he needed support from the Christians around him to help him find new ways to deal with the pain.

It's important to celebrate each small step that someone takes towards a more positive future, whether that be reducing their alcohol and drug dependence, or re-establishing links with estranged families. For some, sleeping rough has become such a way of life that they find it impossible to walk away from it. Tom is seventy and he's been living on the streets for fifteen years. Twice the council have given him a flat but he prefers to sleep on the streets because he feels safer there. That's a decision that those who work with him have to respect. Rather than trying to push him into a home where he doesn't feel comfortable, they try and support him in the place he has chosen to be.

Whilst working with people who have chaotic lifestyles is a privilege, and to be trusted by someone who finds it difficult to trust is an honour, it can also be pretty exhausting. Emily says sometimes progress seems very slow, especially when you see people face painful setbacks. In the midst of that it can be hard for people who work with those who are homeless not to get cynical, especially when they see people falling back into old habits and repeating cycles of unhealthy behaviour. She says it's helpful when the team at the day centre remember to start each day with the prayer that God will help them see each person they come into contact with as his precious son or daughter and that they will treat them accordingly.

That can be our prayer too. Homeless people often say that one of the hardest things about being on the streets is the way people treat them. One guy told me it makes all the difference in the world when people look him in the eye and say hello rather than rushing past, trying to pretend they can't see him. Let's remember that each person who is homeless is a beloved child of God and pray that we would treat them as such in every possible way, holding on to Jesus' words that whatever we do for the person who gets overlooked by others, we do for him (Matthew 25:40, *The Message*).

Chapter 7

War and Peace

A few years ago Mike, one of my team at XLP, was speaking at a church in South London on the importance of engaging with young people.

He asked the congregation if they wanted to see their community change from violence to hope, and as he paused, the church was filled with the sound of someone screaming. A young man stumbled through the church doors, clutching his side with bloody hands. The congregation thought this must be part of a drama sketch and sat patiently waiting to see what would happen next. But Mike hadn't asked anyone to do a drama; this was real.

Mike dropped the microphone and ran to the guy, shouting for others to come and help. Several members of the church applied pressure to the boy's side where he had clearly been stabbed, while Mike tried to calm him – and the increasingly panicked congregation – down. The boy kept saying, "I don't want to die," over and over as they waited for an ambulance and the police to turn up.

They later discovered that the boy was a member of another church and had lost his way whilst travelling to a youth meeting. He asked for directions and another young guy approached him, asking if he knew someone. Though he didn't know the person in question, the guy pulled out a knife and stabbed him. It was completely unprovoked and he could have lost his life just because he lost his sense of direction. The knife went between two ribs, puncturing his lung, but he was taken to hospital and thankfully he survived. Everyone in the church was in shock, particularly those who had looked into the boy's eyes and seen the fear of someone who thinks they are about to die.

That's not the only time Mike has encountered someone who had fallen victim to gang violence. Another time he was driving home with his wife and his brother when they saw a man who had been shot, writhing around on the ground. They jumped out to help, trying to do what they could until an ambulance arrived.

Mike started to apply pressure to the gunshot wound and he realized that though there were many others around, few were actually helping. The friends of the man who had been shot were shouting at everyone (including Mike), and were making the situation even worse. The victim was trying to get them to shut up because they were making him even more scared. Passers-by crossed the road to avoid the situation or drove past as fast as they could with their doors locked. Some well-meaning Christians started shouting "Jesus!" at the tops of their voices at the guy as he was lying on the ground. They didn't come over, ask how they could help or do anything else; they just stood there shouting.

Mike, his wife and his brother all felt totally out of their depth but they chose a different response. They got involved, spoke to the guy, tried to stem the flow of blood, tried to calm him and his friends down and did what they could to help. They couldn't just drive past; this was their community and they knew they had a responsibility to get involved. Mike said that as he looked into the guy's eyes he saw how terrified he was. Any bravado had vanished and as the paramedics arrived and cut away his clothes to better deal with his wound, Mike recognized he was just an ordinary, vulnerable kid who had been forced too early into adulthood.

These two young guys were victims of wars that are being fought across the UK: postcode wars. These wars mean that kids from one area can't enter another area for fear of attack, even if that area is just a few miles from where they live. This is something I've seen in Jamaica where the territories have got smaller and smaller over time, making normal living impossible for gangs confined to these ever-reducing areas. One of the strangest things is that many of those involved don't even know why these postcode wars started in the first place. One young person said to me:

> *I'm from New Cross and there's no way I'd go into Peckham; they'd try to move to me [sic]. You know people's faces and you know who's from your area and who isn't. I don't know how it started. I was born into it and just grew up in it. You're continuing the fight but you don't know what you're fighting for. The kids don't know nothing – they're following Olders who only know a little bit themselves.*

Gangs will protect their territory by any means necessary and young people are frequently killed for being in the wrong area. A police officer has said:

> *There have always been territorial gangs in London. What is different is the level of violence – in most cases knives are used. It is postcode related. I've spoken to young people who say it is about respecting territory. Because they've got nothing else they hold on to what little they've got.*[1]

I've felt increasingly passionate that the church should be right at the heart of bringing peace and reconciliation to communities. After all, peace is at the very heart of the gospel. Jesus was prophesied to be the Prince of Peace (Isaiah 9:6) and he said, "Blessed are the peacemakers, for they will be called sons of God" (Matthew 5:9). Jesus advocated a peaceful response when we're under attack, telling us not to resist but to love our enemies and pray for those who persecute us instead (Matthew 5:38–44). God's kingdom is one of peace, and though we won't see the fullness of the kingdom until Jesus comes again, we should be trying to bring God's kingdom to earth as much as we can.

When I launched my book about gangs, *Fighting Chance*, it seemed right to do it by holding a service for peace. Most of the postcode wars in my area had been between New Cross and Peckham, so we invited a church from New Cross to come to Peckham to have two different churches from very different backgrounds come together to demonstrate unity. Other churches also heard about the idea and got on board. We wanted to highlight to young people in the area that their communities care about them enough to join together across local boundaries. We know that we are stronger together than we are alone and that no single person or organization can tackle this issue successfully; we all need to work together.

Another important element of our service for peace was to stand with those who had lost loved ones through gang violence. One head teacher shared the devastating impact of losing three pupils at her school due to violence. One of the most moving parts of the service was hearing from Barry and Margaret Mizen, whose sixteen-year-old son was killed by a nineteen-year-old boy during an argument in a bakery. Despite their obvious pain, the family have responded by trying to help others. Margaret said:

We go into schools and prisons sharing our story in the hope of changing people. Often we have people listening through their tears, not just for our loss but for the pain and loss of their own lives and the things they have done to hurt others. We want good to come out of something so bad. If something good can come out of the death of our son, then his passing won't have been in vain.

Her husband Barry said:

We want to leave a legacy of peace – for all young people violently murdered in our society. Before this happened we thought the problems of violence weren't our problem, but this affects every one of us. It affects you if you're worried about walking down a street at night or fear for your children. Police and government can't solve this on their own, we can all get involved. Each and every one of us needs to say we want to live in a less violent society. We want to bring a message of hope – a message that change can come.

Sometimes we need to stand in peace, stand in the opposite spirit to the others. During the UK riots in 2011, shop windows in Peckham were smashed in, so owners had to put boards up. A local theatre group wanted to unite the fragile community in a display of peace and remind people of all the positive things about Peckham. So they took over one of the boarded-up shop windows, handed out Post-it notes and pens to passers-by and encouraged them to think about what they love about the area. The idea gathered momentum, people started purposefully heading there to share their thoughts, and soon extra boards were needed. My children and I went to add our voice and to read some of the amazing things people were saying about the area, in contrast to all the negativity that so often surrounds Peckham. It felt as if, in the face of a devastating situation, the community had truly gathered together to remember all the positive things about the people of Peckham. The idea caught the public imagination and soon the story became national and even international news. In the midst of an attack on our streets and our community, the people of Peckham came together and stood proud, reminding the world that you don't overcome hate and anger with more hate and anger. You do it by standing in the opposite spirit of love and peace.

As a church we wanted to do just that and we invited people to join us for another service for peace the Sunday following the riots. Having organized it in only a few days, it was amazing to see the church was absolutely packed full of people. It wasn't just Christians who gathered; many who wouldn't normally come to church came through the doors, wanting to stand together in peace and unity. As part of our worship we took Post-it notes and wrote our prayers for Peckham and our country, expressing our feelings for our community and pinning them to the cross. We encouraged each other to live in the spirit of peace, to love our community and to continue to have hope for our nation.

Northern Ireland

Another place that has suffered much violence is Belfast in Northern Ireland. A few years ago I visited Woodvale Methodist Church, which is situated at the top of the Shankill Road, right at the heart of a Protestant, Loyalist, and working-class community. It is only a few doors away from the Mountain View Tavern which was bombed in 1975, resulting in the loss of five lives. The community has suffered much during the thirty years of the country's "troubles"; they watched the dead bodies dragged out of that pub and have seen people literally blown to pieces around them. I was shocked to see that in some areas that are real hotspots for violence and clashes between marchers, houses often had iron bars across the windows. Some didn't even have windows on the ground floor at all; people had just walled over where the windows should have been to protect themselves.

The community is one of the most deprived areas in the city, with high levels of unemployment, low educational achievement, high levels of addiction to drugs and alcohol and all the social problems associated with many inner cities. Added to that are the trauma and stress of living in fear, not knowing when they might witness, or even fall victim to, yet another tragic sectarian incident. Many people are dependent on anti-depressants and other prescription drugs. It is a community that has lost sight of God with over 95 per cent not having any church connection.

Before I went to Belfast I had heard about the "peace wall", but I was shocked to discover it wasn't just one wall but many. The first one went up in 1969 following rioting and house burnings in west Belfast, and over the years it has risen to more than six metres high. The last one went up just last year in the grounds of an integrated primary school following a period of local tension. Officially there are fifty-three peace lines in four towns and cities in the region; unofficial reports say it may be as many as eighty-eight. It's crazy to see these huge iron barriers that literally cut a community in two, sometimes right in the middle of a street. We talk about divided communities but this is so literal, it forces people apart whether they want to be or not. I found it fascinating that people were just going about their everyday business around the walls. Of course, it's normal to them, but when you see it for the first time it seems very sad that there would be walls separating communities in such a stark way. People living near peace walls sometimes have cages over their back gardens because things get thrown over the walls.

I was told about two nuns who lived either side of one of these huge walls and I loved that simple but definite statement that they were choosing to go against the grain of the division, moving right by the dividing line itself. Most mornings these nuns would find the road littered with bricks and fireworks that had been thrown over the divisions. While they picked up the debris they would pray for peace. You see, for peace to come about, it takes sacrifice. It takes people going against every human instinct and giving of themselves in a way that doesn't make sense to most people. It needs people who will go right to the worst places – the places where they are truly needed – to pick up the debris of violence and fear. It takes people who, in the midst of such troubles, have an unshakable hope in their God and the power of the Holy Spirit. That's the example Jesus showed us. He gave up his position in the heavens and came to where he was most needed, walking amongst the rubble of a broken, hurting world, and loving those who lived in the midst of fear, violence and pain. In all that he said and did he shared his hope of the kingdom of God and in his Father God and in the coming of the Holy Spirit.

One of the amazing nuns who took a stand for peace in Northern Ireland is Sister Bridget. She moved into one of the most troubled communities some years ago with a passion to work in the area in the name of peace. She rented a house just beside a gate on the Protestant side of a fifty-foot peace wall, meaning she was the first in the street to face danger from stones and petrol bombs that were often thrown over the wall. Undeterred, Sister Bridget has lived and worked in this community, bringing together groups from both sides of the divide to discuss and share together. She has been involved in the work of Forthspring, which is an inter-community group working out of the local Methodist church. It has a strong Christian ethos and works alongside both communities to create an environment that seeks to build trust and relationships locally and in the wider society. Among some of its projects, Forthspring is involved in providing after-schools care, works with mums and tots, runs women's groups and supports senior citizens. It has a café space for people to meet and chat. Sister Bridget has been particularly involved in opening up discussions around bringing down the peace walls, and her work has inspired a local author to produce a paper on removing the walls, which is being turned into a play. Her work is effective and getting noticed because she put herself right into the heart of the troubles, became a part of the community and is helping to change it from the inside out.

I had the privilege of meeting members of the Woodvale Church in Shankill, who are longing to bring the peace and love of Jesus to their hurting community. Women from the church reached out to those who weren't part of their congregation and together they have worked on a number of community projects. They saw that many men spent the day in the local pubs and clubs and only stepped out to go to the bookies. They barely ate and were constantly drinking on empty stomachs.

So the group opened up "C'Mon In" and began serving hot meals to the men. I loved the fact that this church weren't judging the men for their drinking; instead they served and blessed them. That, to me, is what grace looks like in action. They have also opened up a café, which is a great centre of the community and provides opportunities for local people to gain skills in the kitchen and behind the counter. David was one man who got involved. His wife left him a few years ago, leading him to turn to drink. Four times he tried to commit suicide and his life seemed to have no purpose. The church asked him to join the "C'Mon In" team and, as a trained chef, David was very comfortable in the kitchen and a real asset to the project. The volunteering gave him purpose again and he said, "This church has given me back my life – it has given me hope." The church leader, a wonderful woman called Margaret, said many have been drawn to participate in an Alpha course through these outreaches. She adds, "We are praying that God will speak to them and that they will come to know that there is a better way – the way of Christ, the way of hope."

Woodvale Church also seeks to break down the tensions between the elderly and the young people in the area. Like many inner-city areas where there is high unemployment, low educational achievement and poor parenting, there is a high level of antisocial behaviour from the young people. This has meant the elderly are fearful of young people, sometimes even of kids as young as five. Working with young people who want to do something positive for their community, the church takes food orders from local residential homes, makes the dinners in the church kitchen and delivers them back to the old people. This project has broken down barriers between the two age groups, demonstrating that not all young people are engaged in antisocial behaviour and helping the young people to really value the elderly in the community.

One of the things I love about the church at large is the ability to do things across generations. I have benefited so much from working with the older generation and learning from their wisdom and experience, yet if it wasn't for the church community, it's unlikely I would have ever connected with them. It's brilliant to see how projects like this can bring

The XLP bus on an estate in London.

XLP's MTV recording studio van at an estate in London.

Children from a Compassion Project in La Paz, Bolivia.

These twins lived in such a poor area that they were brought up being fed dog food

Mixed Opinions, Tower Hamlets Arts Showcase participants who won the XLP Youth Voice Award in 2010 for their song "Child of War".

Sharlene performing outside the XLP bus on an estate in London.

The Arts Showcase Final 2011. Mums ran on stage to embrace their sons after they won the Youth Voice Award.

Left: A playground in LA with four exit points – one leading to the territory of each gang in the area.

Right: Graffiti in Skid Row in downtown LA, which has the largest stable population of homeless people in the USA.

Left: Post it notes in Peckham after the riots in London, Summer 2011.

Right: Peace wall in Northern Ireland's Shankill Road.

Patrick with Aquila and her family in Ghana.

Left: Kofi, one of the children Patrick met in Ghana.

Below: Children in Dampong, Ghana.

Boris Johnson, the Mayor of London, visits the XLP offices in 2011 to discuss the riots that summer.

David Cameron visiting the XLP bus on the Aylesbury estate, South London, in 2010.

Patrick speaking to Nick Robinson, BBC Political Editor.

Bullet Alley, Jamaica. Bullet holes on the side of a house.

Ms Lorna Stanley, who runs Operation Restoration in Trenchtown, Jamaica.

Young people who live in the Geneva refugee camp, Dhaka, Bangladesh, which was set up after the war.

A group of children at the refugee camp in Bangladesh.

XLP community project on an estate in Tower Hamlets, London.

the generations together to bless each other instead of running separate programmes for each age group.

While I was in Northern Ireland, I spoke at a conference where I heard an amazing woman called Kim speak about her experiences of community outreach on the Shankhill Road. I loved how she described her "mission field", showing us slides of the Co-op shop, the local café and the pub. These were the places where she reached out to people, just getting to know them, loving and serving them where they were. Sometimes it's brilliant to remember how simple reaching people can be; it doesn't have to be a huge orchestrated programme of mission and evangelism, but simply living life purposefully. Kim took evening classes as a way to meet and get to know some of the people on challenging estates and has studied other languages so she can reach out to non-English-speaking residents. To be a person who brings about peace in your community, you need to *know* your community and to be seen as part of it, so relationship is always the key. Often we look for the big initiatives to change the world all in one go, but then we become overwhelmed by the size of the problem and any potential solution, and end up never doing anything because we think we'll fail. Kim, however, started at the grass-roots. She joined an evening class. How easy is that? Then she built relationships and helped the people who became her friends. Kim inspired me because she was just trying to bring about peace through her ordinary day-to-day life.

During the troubles churches in the community have obviously been very divided, but now there are signs of hope. I visited the place where the Titanic had been docked many years before. The area around the docks is being redeveloped and currently there are no worship centres on the site. Instead of the usual approach, where each denomination builds its own worship space, the community's vision is that there would be one space shared by all denominations. The plan is to buy a boat that will be docked in the marina where all Christians, Catholic and Protestants alike, can come together for worship, mission and outreach. The project has the support of all denominations, each having nominated someone to sit on the Board of Directors as the project develops. This is an amazing vision for God's people to be united in praise and mission, coming together to bring hope to a city that has been divided along religious lines for far too long.

Praying for peace

Northern Ireland's peace walls are covered in murals. On the Catholic side the images show a clear identification and solidarity with other major conflicts around the world, like the Israel/ Palestine situation and the Spanish Civil War. On the Protestant side there are some harrowing pictures of paramilitary fighters heralded as heroes, men in masks holding machine-guns with words like "Murdered by Cowards" underneath. One of the things that struck me was that the kids in these communities grow up seeing these images every single day. As if the walls themselves weren't enough of a reminder that they are a divided community, these images bring the point home.

Yet many people are using the murals as an opportunity to promote peace. "If Walls Could Talk" began in 2005 and aims to turn a peace wall into one of the longest outdoor art galleries in the world. It gives an opportunity for the community to develop its artistic skills and appreciation of art, as well as raising the debate on the very existence of peace walls in Belfast. Four artists worked closely with a range of local community groups to design murals to replace ten existing paramilitary ones which are a tourist attraction in the area. It's amazing to think the images of violence and pain are being replaced with images symbolizing the hope for peace. You start to see the grass growing in the pavement cracks.

As I stood next to the peace wall I found it hard to know how to pray. My instinct was to pray for the wall to be gone, but it didn't seem as if the communities were ready for that yet. The band U2 wrote a song about an incident in Northern Ireland where British troops shot and killed civil rights protestors, called "Sunday Bloody Sunday". One of the lines in that song talks about trenches in our hearts, meaning the physical things like walls or gang territories that divide communities only exist because we don't allow our hearts to change and let peace and love take root internally. All I could think of was to cry out to God for peace, to pray that he would allow the years of pain and trouble to be healed in people's hearts and in the communities. I could only thank God for the people who are willing to move into such troubled areas and work for peace, bringing God's hope for reconciliation.

If you're an activist like me, you might sometimes find it hard to stop and pray, and instead rush to be getting on with something practical. That's my nature, but I know I need to take time to bring things before God and ask for his wisdom, because I definitely don't have all the answers. Most of the time I don't feel as though I have any answers at all. Praying for peace is something we can all do, whether alone or by bringing our whole community together to pray as one.

The Swiss theologian Karl Barth said:

To clasp the hands in prayer is the beginning of an uprising against the disorder of the world.[2]

And the German theologian Dietrich Bonhoeffer encourages us that praying gives us a different perspective:

> *By praying for such enemies, we do vicariously for them what they cannot do for themselves. Who needs our love more than those who are consumed by hatred? Through prayer we stand beside our enemies and plead to God on their behalf.*[3]

Andrew White, who is known as the Vicar of Baghdad, has seen many of his congregation die due to the war there in Iraq. He has endured threats against his own life many times and lives amongst a people who are in constant fear of what may happen day by day. From a place where becoming a Christian and being baptized has resulted in many losing their lives, he writes:

> *I keep going because I have a hope which is all-embracing, all-consuming, unending and eternal. As long as we who believe in Jesus hold on to hope, we can do anything. There is no such word as "no" in the Christian vocabulary! If we are really following Christ, we hold on to hope and will always achieve that which God has given us to do.*[4]

He points to the fact that God's presence can transform any situation and urges us to look at things through spiritual eyes in order to embrace hope. He says:

> *At this very moment I can look out of my window and see bombed buildings, razor wire, concrete barricades and tanks. The scene presents me with a choice: either I can think, "What a terrible*

place this is" or I can think, "Isn't it wonderful that God has chosen to presence himself here of all places!" Things may look very grim, but with the Almighty everything can change.[5]

How differently would we pray if we re-imagined war-torn places like Northern Ireland as places of peace? Where generations, instead of ignoring each other, start serving each other, where communities that were previously divided come together, and where people under the Spirit of God move into the violent places of the city to stand for peace. God has the power to transform hearts. He can take the parents who are devastated over the loss of a child, and keep them from choosing bitterness and anger. He can turn people's hearts around so that where they were once set on violence and revenge, they seek to live at peace with their enemies. These are the things we can be praying for; this is the hope we have for places of war. These are the beginnings of God's kingdom come – the breaking in of heaven on earth.

Chapter 8
Hope in Ghana

The first time I went to Ghana in West Africa was on a mission trip with a dual purpose of serving and learning more about black history. I wanted to relate better to the kids I was working with from an African culture and I hadn't expected to fall in love with the country in the way that I did. I've since been back many times and now count some of the Ghanaian people as among my best friends. From the first moment I set foot in the country, I felt so welcome, probably because forty people from the church congregation turned up at the airport! They surrounded our small group singing, "I love you with the love of the Lord." From that moment on they drew us into their community with an infectious sense of joy, but it didn't take long for me to see that there was a lot of pain behind their smiles.

I learned some of the horrific history of the country, visiting the prisons where thousands of slaves were kept before being shipped off to America or the Caribbean. The whitewashed buildings seem pretty innocuous from the outside but as you step in, you find out how inhumane the conditions were. Tiny underground dungeons were literally crammed with men, women and children, sometimes around 1,000 of them in a space where even 150 would feel squashed. There was no light or air for the slaves, some were chained to the walls, and the only respite was half an hour a day when they were released to walk in the courtyard. There were no toilet facilities for them so they had no choice but to go where they stood. Over the 200 years in which prisoners were kept in these conditions, the floor level was raised by two feet by such waste matter. Anyone who survived the ordeal of the dungeons was stripped down and sent off on ships, where the conditions were often even worse. It's not clear how many faced this fate but it's estimated that it was between 12 million and 25 million over the 200 years of the slave trade. It's so hard to comprehend how these atrocious acts could have happened and it's almost impossible to imagine how people lived through such abuse. What's even harder to digest is that one of the first British churches in Ghana was built above one of these very dungeons; Christians sang of a loving God while their fellow man suffered below.

Sadly, the country's difficulties aren't limited to the past. Ghana is Africa's second largest producer of gold and supplies 15 per cent of the world's cocoa. It should be well off but instead it suffers from terrible poverty thanks to the corrupt governments of the 1960s and 1970s. Some village chiefs are still dishonest; they sell off land and pocket the money without reinvesting it in the community. There's actually enough food for everyone to eat in Ghana, but it doesn't get to people because there isn't an infrastructure to collect food and distribute it to where it's needed. Many villages don't have electricity and feel forgotten about because aid often arrives in the big cities but doesn't make it out to them. Sometimes missionaries have come along and promised to change things and get electricity supplies hooked up, only to disappear and never be seen again.

I've visited many villages to try and get a picture of what life is like in the country. As I chatted to young people in these villages it has quickly become clear that there is very little for them to do. Most villages have a very small bar, a primary school and a church. That's it. Even the younger children miss a lot of school, as the school buildings aren't designed to withstand the weather and so are shut for weeks at a time after a storm until they are rebuilt and ready to be used again. Most of the young people are extremely bored, many start sleeping around, and inevitably there are teenage pregnancies as a result. At the end of primary school, most kids leave education to help their parents work the land. Others leave the village to head for the nearest city where they can earn more money to be sent back to the family.

One young guy said to me, "It's hard to dream when you have no support," and I could see what he meant. It's hard to have hope when there are few opportunities and virtually no alternatives to walking in your parents' footsteps. They look ahead and all they see is a long hard slog to stay alive; they have no role models showing them that life can be any different.

Alcohol is also a huge problem, again often driven by boredom. Many of the villages make their own alcohol, meaning it's cheap but potentially very dangerous, as it can contain a lethal cocktail.

Prostitution is becoming a much bigger problem; people have nothing to sell, so they sell their bodies. Many of the men have numerous girlfriends and for these girls, that's the only way to survive. They don't believe they could ever do anything themselves as they have no education and can't read and write. What hope is there for their future? They just hang on to the guy, hoping he'll look after them. There is little understanding of contraception and consequently many women go from pregnancy to pregnancy. Often the church and missionaries have taught women in places like Ghana that contraceptives are wrong and that if you use a condom you will burn in hell. Yet it's hard to comprehend that teaching when men are sleeping around, contracting HIV and then passing it on to their wives.[1] The women pass it on to unborn babies, or children through breast-feeding. Lack of contraception is costing people their lives, and communities are paying dearly for it. I'm not suggesting for one minute we support the practice of people sleeping around, but we need to think about the messages we give out. Women can't afford to provide for their kids, some even turn to prostitution to be able to buy food for them, so having more babies isn't going to help. There's a huge need for education and support over and above judgmental opinions.

Ghana's children

The children of Ghana have always had a massive impact on me. There are so many heartbreaking stories; it seems as though everywhere you turn there's another need, another child whose life you can't comprehend. Kofi always springs to mind because although he was eleven when we first met him, he was so badly malnourished that he was about the same size as his five-year-old brother. He suffers from digestive problems, causing him to throw up after he's eaten. At first we tried giving his mum some money so she could take him to the hospital and get help, but later we discovered she had spent the money on alcohol instead. It's hard to judge her, given how painful her life is and knowing that she is addicted to alcohol, but it's heartbreaking to see Kofi's weak body and know how much he's suffering. On one of our visits we were able to take him to hospital ourselves, but we always know that ultimately we're getting on a plane and we have to leave him there to cope with a difficult stomach condition and an alcoholic mother.

It's always heartbreaking to meet parents who have lost children through preventable diseases, and the sad truth is that in a country like Ghana people don't just lose one child that way, they lose many. I've got to know a woman called Elizabeth, who has lost seven children to preventable diseases. Seven. There can be few things in life as painful as burying your own child, and she'd had to do that seven times, when each child could have lived had there been access to the right prevention or medicine. During one of our visits to Elizabeth she asked us to visit one of her surviving grandsons, Daniel, in hospital. The conditions were appalling. There were flies everywhere, it was stiflingly hot and the mattresses didn't even have sheets on them. Daniel was hooked up to an IV that had a line drawn across the bag. We asked what it meant and were told that when the fluids reached the line, Daniel's money had run out and he would be sent home. Without the fluids he would die quickly. When we asked how much more it would cost to treat him, it turned out to be just a few pounds. We were able to help Daniel, saving Elizabeth from having to bury another child, but were frightened to think of how many other children there were like him around the country, dying for the sake of so little money.

Whilst many children are in homes where they are loved and valued, others are seemingly thrown by the wayside. We met one boy who had been born as the result of his mother's affair and so he was excluded from their family. He was given to his aunt to look after, though she barely had enough money to keep her own children alive. Another boy was born cross-eyed and as a result his mum said he wasn't worth wasting her money on, so she wouldn't pay for him to go to school. We met a sweet two-year-old girl called Gifted whose legs were bent; she couldn't talk at all and seemed to have problems with her eyes as well. Her mother had abandoned her to the care of her elderly grandmother, who refused to acknowledge there was anything wrong with her. I walked away from that home feeling so angry and confused about all that I was seeing; it broke my heart to know that Gifted had been rejected because she wasn't perfect and it was unlikely she'd ever get the medical help she needed.

So many times I've just felt absolutely overwhelmed by situations like these and the sheer scale of poverty that I've seen. It's so hard to be in the midst of people who have so little and know there's only a limited amount that you can do. At the end of one meeting when we'd offered to pray for anyone who was sick, a mother pressed her son into my arms. He weighed almost nothing and I didn't need a doctor to tell me how ill he was. His cheeks were hollow, his eyes glazed, his body was so thin that his arms were only as thick as two of my fingers. We got him to hospital that night but six months later we heard that he had died.

Another time we went to a village and almost immediately were surrounded by people's needs. They pushed around the team, wanting to touch us, asking us for money, needing prayer; it was all too much. We felt we had so little to give them and were overwhelmed. We stopped right where we were and began to worship God in song. We had to turn to him and remind ourselves we were just trying to serve in his name. We couldn't do everything but just by praising God the atmosphere changed. People calmed down and we were able to spend hours in the village praying with people for their various needs.

Since my first trip to Ghana I've wanted to do more than bring short-term relief to these problems; I want to see places transformed and see long-term change. I've sometimes struggled in Ghana with being perceived as the white man who comes and gives handouts, and I don't want that reputation. I want to find a way for people to feel empowered to help themselves, because handouts only provide a temporary fix. I want people to start lifting their eyes, raising their hope and seeing all sorts of possibilities for their future.

I've been privileged to get to know some amazing people

in Ghana, one of whom is Pastor Akousa. She works in the Ashanti Akim region, where she pastors a number of churches and runs a charity that works to improve education and health for the local population of around 95,000. Her own life was filled with despair because of a bad marriage until she met with Jesus and experienced the healing power of his love. She was so impacted by God's love that she believed there was nothing he couldn't do. That fuelled her to seek the same love and transformation for others.

She has a passion to help the Ghanaian people see that with a bit of support, they can be the answer to the challenges in their community. I spoke to her about my desire to see change and to find out the best way to help, and she told me education is the key. Pastor Akousa was brought up in a village called Dampong where, like many places in poverty, aspiration is low and there is a general acceptance that life will always be the same way. She said that there are only three secondary schools in the entire region and the creation of more is key to long-term change.

A school sounded like the perfect thing for us to be involved in, so we started making plans. We asked the village chief if he would provide the land, knowing it was important that the village owned the project and actively bought into it rather than feeling it was something we were just doing for them. He gave us thirty-two acres and told us if we needed more, it was ours. The land he gave us was like a jungle; it was overgrown and looked as if it would never be turned into anything. I'm always saying to my team that vision is the art of seeing the invisible, so this was an occasion for us all to practise! We walked together down the dusty track and tried to imagine that rather than desolate wasteland ahead of us, there was a fantastic school that was able to accommodate a hundred kids. It would be sturdy and built to withstand the weather, with real toilets and a football pitch. I told everyone to imagine a group of children, no longer in tatty, worn clothes but proudly wearing their new school uniforms. I asked them to see past the weeds to how the school could bring the community together, giving them hope and vision for their future. To be honest, the team probably thought I'd lost the plot, but I knew that for us to really get behind the vision, we needed to see past how things were and see what they could be instead.

The community pitched in and helped with the building work. We sent teams over from the UK to help and raised money to fund the project. It took a few years and a lot of hard work, but in 2007 the school opened and those visions became reality. It opened with three new classrooms and there are plans for five more, plus workshops and more sports facilities. The school has become known as the place where "even the poor can get educated" and that's exactly what we hoped for. It will also have an eye clinic attached that provides medical services as well as vital healthcare information that is almost impossible for people to access elsewhere. When I spoke to the young people attending the school and asked them what they wanted to do with their lives, they replied, "I want to farm the land," or "I want to be a doctor." Others told me they wanted to be a teacher, work in a bank or be an airline pilot. "I want to be the first in my family to graduate," others told me. It was incredible to see the glimmer of hope in their eyes as they talked about their future – a future that was suddenly wide open and full of possibilities. With each visit the school grows stronger and I meet more and more kids who have hope because they now have a chance of a brighter future.

As I said, it's easy to get overwhelmed by so many needs and the painful reality is that we can't change every situation in Ghana. On a recent visit I spent some time with Aquila, whom I met on my first visit, when her son was very sick in the hospital.

Because he was the same age as my own son, seeing him became particularly poignant and every time I've been back to the country I've made sure I have some time with them. Aquila showed me a photo we'd had taken on that first visit where one of Aquila's daughters had been sat on my lap and her young son was standing beside me. Both had since died. She pointed to others from the community in the picture who had also lost their lives. It was devastating to see those beautiful, smiling faces looking up at me from a picture, knowing we hadn't been able to do enough to help them. If we could have got them more medical help or cleaner drinking water, they might be running round my feet instead of buried in the ground. When I looked into Aquila's eyes I couldn't comprehend all the pain and suffering she'd lived through. Despair was written all over her face and I felt sick to my stomach.

Yet when I look at the kids in the school I can see that there is hope. We can't do everything by any means, but we can't let that stop us from achieving the things we can do. Sometimes we'll have the joy of seeing lives changed, other times we'll know the tragedy of lives being needlessly lost. We can't plaster on a happy smile and pretend we'll sort everything out in an instant. We have to be prepared for the heartaches and allow them to spur us on to achieve more. I couldn't save Aquila's children, but I could be a part of a team that set up a school, leaving a legacy of hope amongst the community, allowing them to see that change is possible.

The end of poverty

Everyone has a different calling when it comes to these issues because everyone has different skills and gifts to bring. Mohammed Yunas was an economics professor from Bangladesh, one of the poorest nations in the world. In 1996 he lent money to forty-two women in a village near the university. Previously these women had only been able to borrow money from loan sharks who charged high interest rates because they had nothing to offer by way of a guarantee on a loan. With Mohammed Yunas's small loans they were able to work, generate incomes and improve their families' lives. Around ten years later Grameen Bank had been established by Yunas, with 20,000 workers lending $800 million a year to 6.6 million members nationwide.[2] Amazingly, 99 per cent of clients were able to pay their loans back: all they needed was someone to give them a chance in the first place. This simple but highly effective micro-credit model earned Yunas the title "the world's banker for the poor" and the Nobel Peace Prize in 2006.

Yunas used what he knew to empower people and give them what they needed to get themselves out of poverty. Sometimes the loans were just a few dollars but they made all the difference in the world. His vision is to eradicate poverty to the extent that by 2030 we'll be creating poverty museums so children will be able to see how the world used to look. What an incredible vision for the future; imagine having to take your children or grandchildren to a museum to learn about poverty and deprivation because they were things that no longer existed for them to see in the world around them. Imagine how it would feel to know that poverty was in our past and not in our future. That blows me away and that's a vision that casts hope and propels us all to act to make it a reality.

When you talk about the end of poverty, Christians often quote Jesus' words from Mark 14:7: "The poor you will always have with you." It seems to be one of the most misunderstood verses and for many it has become an excuse not to fight poverty. If we believe that Jesus was really saying there is no chance of defeating poverty, we're dead in the water. As Dr Scott Todd, an expert on global poverty, says, "Where low expectations are fuelled by misapplied scripture, hell must be pleased."[3] When we put this one verse into the context of a whole Bible that has over 2,000 verses about God's heart for the poor, it just doesn't make sense. Time and time again God spoke to the prophets, telling them to remind his people to look after the poor. How could a God who is so passionate and so vocal about addressing poverty say, "Don't worry too much about the poor, they'll always be around"? It just doesn't make sense.

Let's take a closer look at the context of what Jesus said, looking at the story as it's told in Mark 14, John 12 and Luke 7. The scene is quite famous: it's where Mary, sister of Lazarus, comes to anoint Jesus at the house of Simon the Leper, who many believe had been healed by Jesus. That would mean Simon was no longer a leper who was isolated from the rest of society, but was able to hold a party in his own house with the Messiah in attendance; quite a reason to celebrate! Added to this, Lazarus – who had not long been raised from the dead – was also there. Again, a good reason to celebrate! There must have been a huge sense of anticipation and excitement and wonder about what else Jesus might do. Wouldn't meeting someone who'd been brought back to life raise your faith level and expectations?

In contrast, the whole evening must have been overshadowed for Jesus by the fact that he was getting ever nearer to facing the cross. Mary came into the house and poured out an extravagantly expensive perfume on Jesus. Judas was quick to complain, saying it was a waste and that the money could have been given to the poor. Jesus looked between Mary, who had done something so beautiful and special to him, and Judas, who was responding angrily, and told Mary she had done a good thing. He said to Judas, "You will always have the poor among you, but you will not always have me." What is absolutely vital is that we know that Jesus was talking to Judas and not to the whole of mankind at this point. He wasn't laying down a mandate for the eternal continuation of poverty; he was speaking to one of his disciples whose heart was hard.

This is key for us to grasp both for ourselves and for others around us who quote that one verse and forget about the thousands of other verses telling us to spend ourselves on behalf of the poor. We can't afford to misinterpret Jesus' words, to sit back and do nothing while people die from starvation and preventable diseases, when the food and medicine to keep them alive are available. We know God's desire is for his people to do what they can to bring his kingdom to earth today; his heart cries out for the poor. We need to look at the fact that we *are* stamping out poverty and injustice in our world today and find encouragement and motivation from that change to keep going. The number of people living in extreme poverty has been halved in the last thirty years – could we bring that figure down to zero if we truly believed that it was possible?

Dr Scott Todd says that the biggest reason the poor are still with us is because we expect that they should be. We need hope that our world can be dramatically different; we need to be released from our low expectations.[4] If we start to believe that God doesn't want poverty, we begin to have hope again, hope that our world can change, and hope that there is another way. When we allow that hope to be released in our hearts, we start to be inspired, re-imagining how the world could be. As we allow God to increase that hope and combine it with hearts full of his compassion, we are motivated to play our part and do something to see the end of extreme poverty.

Chapter 9

Hope for People with Addictions

F igures suggest that our society is becoming increasingly dependent on alcohol and drugs.

Alcohol consumption has doubled in the last fifty years and grown by 15 per cent in the last five years alone. The most worrying development is that the age of people drinking seems to be getting lower, with the number of children consuming alcohol doubling over recent years. An enormous 45 per cent of 14–15 year-olds drink on a regular basis and one in ten 16–24 year-olds say they have used drugs in the last month. Cocaine is used by twice as many people as it was seven years ago and the number of deaths it causes has gone up by 300 per cent in five years. It's not just our inner cities that are struggling; alcohol and drugs are increasingly becoming big problems in rural areas too.

Debates have raged about the reasons for this increase. It's too easy to say it's because of the availability of cheap alcohol, lack of drug controls, increased peer pressure, and young people's desire to experiment. More considered research suggests that the real reasons are poor parenting, lack of supervision, parents who are drug addicts or alcoholics themselves, unhappy childhoods, and people trying to escape the pain and trauma of their lives.

Adrian and Jane

I was determined to explore further how God can work through us to help those who are addicted. I took a trip to South-East Asia to see the work of my friends Adrian and Jane, with their children Tim and Ann, whom I'd known from my church in London. They had uprooted their entire lives, left everything they knew, had to start again in an entirely different culture, and they were doing it all to serve people with serious addictions.

Adrian and Jane centre their programme around family life, giving each recovering addict a strict routine that is rooted in prayer and dependence on God, and household chores. They see the process as like parenting a baby. During the addicts' first ten days in the house they are considered to be like a newborn, which needs to be allowed to cry out for help and just be loved in return. As the person with an addiction starts to recover their strength, they usually start acting more like a toddler, who rebels against the authority of the house, pushing their "parents" away to try to assert their independence and test the boundaries created for them. If they progress beyond this stage, they start setting boundaries for themselves as they move on towards independence. They use no medication to take the edge off the drug withdrawals; the only treatment is prayer. For the first week or so they will have someone with them praying constantly both in their local language and in tongues, and after this time prayer continues to be a key part of their day.

This was no nine-to-five job; they lived together with the addicts in order to provide a positive role model of what it means to be family. From what I could see, that seemed to me a key part of the healing process, especially as many people with addictions are rejected and disowned by their families. It can be the loneliest and most desperate time in someone's life when they're trying to get clean and they find they have pushed away most of the people who loved them. With people like Adrian and Jane they are part of a family again; they are loved and cared for through thick and thin.

Adrian and Jane told me that they take a long-term view of rehab, knowing it can take many years for someone to truly come off drugs. Adrian explained that hope is something that needs to be nurtured in the addicts and they need to be shown the possibilities for their lives one step at a time. I found that very challenging because our culture is so focused on getting instant results. The average time a person in the UK stays in a youth work job is two years, nowhere near long enough to see someone through rehab. It also shows the sacrificial nature of this work – spending maybe five to ten years walking through the highs and lows of investing in each person. It may seem relatively easy getting somebody off drugs to start with, but it takes a lot of dedication, perseverance and energy to help them continue to grow above and beyond their threshold of addiction.

Prayer is vital because these people have usually been badly hurt and need healing from those pains to be able to deal with the resulting addiction. They have to deal with the root causes that got them addicted in the first place so they can stay off drugs. Adrian says that many of the addicts they work with believe that they are nothing, they have no sense of self-worth and they need Jesus to speak truth into their lives. As they pray through situations from the past, they ask Jesus to come into those areas and bring healing.

As an example, Adrian told me about a guy who, when he was a boy, was held down on the hearth and beaten repeatedly by his father for putting a scratch on the family bicycle. This beating left him in agony. As they prayed with him, they asked him to imagine Jesus coming into the situation and to picture what he would do. The guy said, "Jesus would have taken me away from the hearth and looked after me." They helped him to understand the lie he had taken on board from his dad's behaviour (that he was worthless and deserved to be punished), and then they could pray with him that he would know the truth that Jesus loved him and that he didn't deserve what had happened to him. Many of the people Adrian and Jane's group meet have these deep-seated and false beliefs about themselves that can be traced back to incidents in their childhood that have caused them pain. Working as a team, they try and strip everything else away so they can get to the real root of the problem and the person can receive the healing of Jesus. It's incredible to hear about the change that comes as a result and humbling to see their dependence on prayer. It's not a last resort – it's their only resort. They realize that for the people they are working with it's the love of God that will transform their hearts.

Whilst they're seeing people set free from addictions and going on to lead normal lives, of course there are also stories of those who don't make it. Adrian hesitates to point to "success" stories because he knows all too well that someone who is doing well one year might hit a brick wall the next. I asked Adrian how the family cope with the disappointment of seeing someone come so far then fall back, and he told me that each time it happens they really go through a grief process. It's hard for Adrian and the team to hold people lightly – after all, each addict who comes into the programme is essentially invited to join their family life.

Sometimes people are with them for years, then something happens and they go back to their old way of life. One woman, June, lived with them for six and a half years, joining them in their family flat when their daughter Ann was just six.

Within the first year June had discovered that she was HIV positive and had been so grateful that her "adopted family" had been so accepting and caring as her health started to deteriorate. Recently, however, June had unprotected sex and became pregnant, and then had a back-street abortion. Rather than facing the situation, June decided to leave, much to the disappointment of Adrian and his family. Of course, for June and the other "family members" who've left over the years, it's definitely not the end of the story, but it's still painful to say goodbye in circumstances like those.

I asked Adrian how he and Jane find the strength to carry on when they have such heartbreaking setbacks. He said he learned at the start that it was never going to be a smooth process. In the early days they got to know a group of people who changed and grew over five years, before they started dropping out one by one and left them feeling devastated. People who'd been working with addicts for much longer told him the only thing they could do was just keep bringing everything back to Jesus – whether their hopes for a person, or their pain that they didn't make it. They told them to "keep the great commandment before the great commission" – meaning we're to love Jesus and people first and foremost, before we try and make them disciples. Adrian said trying to love without any agenda has been a huge part of the learning process for them. Usually we love people because we think we'll receive love in return, but when someone is not in a place where they are capable of giving us that, we have to love them anyway. Adrian warned too that it's easy when working with people in such situations to find yourself going into "rescuer mode", and he said it's something they have to guard against all the time.

"We want to enable people to live freer lives, not get into a co-dependent relationship with them," he said. "When you meet someone with an addiction you have to remember that his or her needs can only be met by Jesus; you'd burn yourself out if you tried to do it yourself."

The church family that has come into being since Adrian and Jane moved into their city can't worship publicly because of the country's political restrictions; Christian leaders can be arrested and interrogated for holding such "illegal" meetings. I'd never been to an underground church meeting and I had no idea what to expect. The thing that blew me away was how people worshipped. It was extraordinary to be amongst people I knew to be recovering addicts, seeing them so dependent on God's Spirit, calling out to him, knowing how much they needed him to come through for them. I was almost jealous of that desperation. It seemed to me that all of us should be fully dependent on God to help us, whether we are addicts or not.

As part of their meeting they had a time for people to tell their stories and it was very emotional to hear about the amazing things God had done in people's lives. Ben told us he'd been on heroin for ten years before he got free. Although his father was a government official, he'd been sentenced for GBH when he was eighteen and had the all-too-familiar story of learning the prison/crime culture before his release. As his lifestyle went from bad to worse he ended up in a local methadone centre. His father had officially disowned him and his marriage was just about finished. Hearing from Adrian and the team about how Jesus could give him a new life, he decided to give Jesus a try. A year later he not only found he was getting free of drugs, but he'd opened his home for people to come and meet this Jesus too. Today he and his wife run a café where others in the programme are finding themselves on the way to recovery from addictions.

That evening I also saw a woman who'd come to the meeting for the first time. Adrian told me that, when they'd visited her in the local methadone centre, he'd been asked to pray for her baby, who had been born addicted to heroin. As the mother transferred onto the methadone, she had stopped breast-feeding – leaving the baby to go through "cold turkey". The baby was crying hysterically until it was placed in Adrian's arms. Touched by the Holy Spirit, the baby fell into a peaceful sleep.

The thing that really struck me about people who work with addicts is that there are no half measures. What seems to work best is when the person with an addiction is invited to be part of, and embraced by, a community that really lives life together, learns together, struggles together, cries together and laughs together. That's what I saw in South-East Asia and I've seen it in other projects around the world. This is the kind of community we, as followers of Jesus, are meant to be. We're meant to be a people who love unconditionally, without agenda or limits; people who will make themselves totally vulnerable for the sake of another. We should love others with all our hearts and persevere with them through the heartbreak, hurt and setbacks; and commit to keep on loving despite all the odds. We're meant to be people who will stand with others in their worst nightmares and pray with the passion we can normally only generate when it's for someone we love. How do we know that this is what the people of God should do? Because it's what God does for us and demonstrated so incredibly through Jesus.

Limits on our love

A challenge for us all to overcome is our desire to have limits on our love. We try to protect ourselves by setting up limits on the extent we will love others; we can do it almost instinctively to help us feel secure and safe, but we must challenge ourselves to love unconditionally and without limits. An encounter between Jesus and a lawyer, that we read about in Luke 10, shows our instinct to put limits on our love. An expert in the law stood up and challenged Jesus to tell him what he had to do to inherit eternal life. Jesus' reply, as usual, didn't answer the question directly. Instead he said, "What is written in the Law?" The lawyer replied, "'Love the Lord your God with all your heart and with all your soul and with all your strength and with all your mind'; and, 'Love your neighbour as yourself.'" What an incredible statement! No caveats, no limitations, no agendas – just love with everything you have. But the lawyer did what we are so often tempted to do: he tried to set some limits by asking, "Who is my neighbour?" Jesus' response was to tell the story of the Good Samaritan. Although thinking of Samaritans today conjures up images of amazingly kind people who can be phoned when someone is in desperate need, in Jesus' day the Samaritans were loathed and despised by the Israelites and the feelings were pretty much mutual from the Samaritans' point of view. At the end of the story, Jesus asked the lawyer, "[Who] do you think was a neighbour to the man who fell into the hands of robbers?" The Jewish lawyer, embarrassed, had to admit it was the Israelite victim's worst enemy – the Samaritan. Jesus was telling the lawyer, the crowd and us that the limit to the question, "Who should I love as myself?" is "Even your worst enemy!" *There are no limits!*

Take another well-known story, the Prodigal Son, or as it might perhaps be better called, the Parable of the Father. The son had insulted and hurt his father by asking for his inheritance even before the father was dead. He spent the money on a sex, drugs and rock and roll lifestyle, and eventually found himself in the worst, most disgusting, most culturally unacceptable job – living with and feeding pigs. In first-century Palestine, this story told of the worst sinner on the planet, as far as the listeners were concerned. Yet, in the midst of all of this, the sinner decided to return home to his father. As in so many of Jesus' stories, our natural thought process may lead us to believe that the returning son deserved nothing but judgment, condemnation and punishment for his terrible actions. But instead, Jesus says, the father ran towards his son, threw his arms around him and kissed him. He didn't even stop there. He put his best robe on the son's filthy and dishevelled body, and threw a party to celebrate his returning to the family. There were no limits to the love the father felt for his child. The son had done just about the worst thing that he could do to the father, the family, others and himself, but the father did not draw a line, as we are often tempted to do, and say, "You've gone too far, you are too bad, you are not worth helping." He demonstrated God's heart that there are no limits to love.

This is the amazing news of the gospel: our God places no limits on his love for us. No one has ever been, or will ever be, considered "too bad" for God to love them. He loves each of us without agenda. Even if we break his heart by not loving him back or by doing the most sinful things, he carries on loving us just the same. Jesus showed us and taught us that because of his love, we are free to love others this way too. We are able, in the power of God's Holy Spirit, to love in a way that we never knew was possible. People are desperate to be loved. Loneliness is one of the biggest problems in the world. If you walk into the average pub, you'll find people sitting alone, nursing a drink. They could have chosen to drink at home, but often loneliness leads them to sit in a pub where they can feel as though they are in the company of others, even if they don't speak to anyone. There are people living near my family who I have seen become isolated as they get older because their spouse has died, their friends have moved away, or they are less able to get around. Other people I know struggle with any sense of self-worth because of what they have done in the past, or often what was done to them. They live with the ever-present thought of "Why would God, or anyone else, ever love me?" There are those who are living with terrible illnesses or the sickness of a loved one for many years. The list is endless of the people out there who find themselves beyond our self-made limits of love. Mother Teresa said that loneliness is the greatest disease in our world, with people feeling as if they just don't matter to anyone. Is it any surprise, then, how many people turn to drugs and alcohol when faced with such emptiness in their hearts?

The good news of the gospel is twofold: firstly, the good news for us is that the bondage of our self-made limits to our love is broken and we are set free to love in a whole new way. When you embrace that, it will change your life forever. Secondly, the good news for those who are considered the last, the least and the lost is that we as God's people are coming to love the hell out them – to love them like the Father loves them and to show them a glimpse of heaven's love in the here and now that will change not only their life here on earth, but their eternity. Now that's good news. The theologian Jürgen Moltmann said:

> *A closed human being no longer has any hope. Such a person is full of anxiety. A closed society no longer has a future. It kills the hope for life of those on its periphery, and then it finally destroys itself. Hope is lived, and it comes alive when we go outside of ourselves and, in joy and pain, take part in the life of others.*[1]

We are a people of hope and we need to let our hope in the gospel and our God come alive. But we will only do so when we are willing to do as Moltmann urges us and "go outside of ourselves and, in joy and pain, take part in the life of others".

Living this way speaks to people's hearts about the gospel we so desperately want to share. The early church had its share of challenges and problems, as Paul's letters testify, but they made a hugely disproportionate impact on their local communities and on large areas of the known world. Michael Green said of the early church:

They made the grace of God credible by a society of love and mutual care which astonished pagans and was recognized as something entirely new. It lent persuasiveness to the claim that the new age had dawned in Christ. The word was not only announced but seen in the community of those who were giving it flesh... Here love was given daily expression; reconciliation was actually occurring... the weak were protected, the stranger welcomed. People were healed, the poor and dispossessed were cared for and found justice.[2]

Humility is crucial to living like this. Humility sets you free to love in the way that Jesus loves. Humility isn't something you can conjure up but is a natural outworking of your relationship with the Father, the Son, and the Holy Spirit. Our society is driven by fame and there is something in us all that craves to be recognized for what we do. It might just be on a small scale, where we simply want a pat on the back for doing a good job, or perhaps it's far bigger and we are desperate to be "somebody" in the eyes of other people around us.

If we seek recognition we are serving with an agenda, and again the act of looking for a return on our love places limits on the way we can love people. Philippians 2:6–8 describes the very essence of Jesus' expression of love for us: "being in very nature God... [he] made himself nothing, taking the very nature of a servant... he humbled himself and became obedient to death – even death on a cross!" We're told to echo our Saviour's attitude: "Do nothing out of selfish ambition or vain conceit, but in humility consider others better than yourselves. Each of you should look not only to your own interests, but also to the interests of others" (verses 3–4).

This means we love and serve, letting go of our need for recognition and congratulations for how well we're doing. As Brian McLaren said:

> *This language of the secrecy resonates with the entire message of Jesus. His kingdom is not about a show. It's not about high volume and hype, glitzy spectacle, or impressive appearances. No, the reverse: it is understated, secret, behind the scenes. Its rewards come not through public talk but though potent, private practice.*[3]

Following Jesus sometimes means serving in the hidden places and loving people who don't love us back. It means giving to people who will never give back to us in the same way – whether that's because of an addiction or any other reason. It means serving people who may let us down, get angry with us and ultimately walk away from us. Following Jesus means we choose to do it anyway. We do it for the love of our Saviour and for the glory of his kingdom. We entrust people into his hands and know that we just need to be faithful to him and his ways.

God asks us to give all we have, even if we feel as though

we have very little. That always brings to mind the story of the widow's offering in Mark 12:41–44. When the woman put her two coins in the Temple offering she made no fuss, and we don't hear of her trying to draw a crowd to see her sacrifice. Instead Jesus, who had just been scolding the crowd about excessive displays of power and arrogance, commends her and tells us we should follow her example. No one else would have even given her a second look, but Jesus noticed her genuine offering of all she had, and he wanted us to know he'll see us when we make the same offerings with our lives. The things we do in loving and caring for others may not feel powerful or dramatic, spectacular or revolutionary, but there is great power in doing things not for our own need for recognition, but through a love for God and people and a passion to see God's kingdom come. This is the hope of the gospel of Jesus.

It doesn't end there, because there's even more good news! In Isaiah 58 we find that when we begin to live like this, God says:

> *Your lives will begin to glow in the darkness, your shadowed lives will be bathed in sunlight. I will always show you where to go. I'll give you a full life in the emptiest of places... You'll use the old rubble of past lives to build anew... You'll be known as those who can fix anything... make the community livable again...*
>
> Isaiah 58:9–12, *The Message*

What amazing promises! As we love without limits and give of ourselves, we find hope for those whom many would write off and we find hope for our own lives too. We realize again that there is no ceiling to hope in God's kingdom.

Chapter 10
Hope in Politics

U ntil recent years I had absolutely no interest in politics whatsoever.

I always thought it was something for intellectual people and I certainly wouldn't class myself as one of those. At school I was Mr Average at most things and in fact the only thing I excelled in was sport. I started playing football for a local team, Colchester, and had the opportunity to turn professional when I was sixteen. I lacked confidence, though, and didn't believe I was good enough, so I went to college instead, and a few years later started XLP.

As it turned out, by starting XLP I was to some extent stepping into the political arena. We were dealing with political issues like education, family breakdown and crime, and we even got to know our local MP, Simon Hughes, pretty well. I respected Simon because he would often come along to XLP events and give us his support; it was clear that he was passionate about helping people in the community, so it always felt as if we were on the same page. Aside from our interactions with Simon, though, I continued to avoid politics, still convinced it was only for people far brighter than I was.

Then, a few years ago, I received an invitation, completely out of the blue, to speak at the Conservative Party annual conference. I was stunned and petrified. Not only did I have no idea why they would want me to speak at their conference, I found out they wanted me to speak on the main stage, which would be broadcast live on TV. Every insecurity I had ever had reared its ugly head: What could I possibly say? Would I even be able to understand what everyone else was talking about? Wouldn't I make myself look stupid? I thought I was bound to get something wrong. I'd never claimed to be clever but I was seized with fear that people would see me, think I was completely stupid, and it would destroy any trust they had in me. I reasoned that there were loads of people around me who were far more capable and intelligent. They should be speaking rather than me.

I'm something of a perfectionist, so of course I absolutely hate making mistakes. Being on a stage in front of thousands of people, and on live TV, talking about something I felt unqualified to talk about, gave me the potential for making a lot of mistakes. I knew that whatever I said, I would be criticized; constructive and not-so-constructive criticism seemed par for the course in the world of politics. I was sorely tempted to say no and walk away so that I was in no danger of embarrassing myself. Then I began to wonder how many other challenges my nagging self-doubts had led me to shy away from. I realized that any good things I'd been involved in, I had put down to being a fluke, and if people told me I was doing a good job I figured they were just being nice or saying it because they liked me. I felt I had "got away with it" in the past, but that if I did this, my true colours would come out and people would realize who I really was.

My head was a minefield of new and terrifying thoughts. Why should I be the one to speak to the Conservative Party conference? What did I have to say? I'd faced a lot of challenges working with young people and travelling to different countries, but this felt totally different. I was more insecure about this than I had been about mediating between gang leaders. My wife is a life coach and she said I was dealing with "imposter syndrome", meaning that deep down I felt like a fraud. That was me to a "T". But I couldn't walk away from this God-given opportunity because of my insecurity. I had a few months to prepare for the conference and as I prayed and talked about my doubts, I knew I had to trust in God. I had to hold on to the fact that he is enough for me and that in everything I need to lean on him, not on my own strength.

I arrived at the conference hoping I looked more confident than I felt. I still didn't feel as though I fitted in, especially when I realized I was almost the only person in the room not wearing a suit. A couple of guys from my team came with me and, to their great amusement, I was asked to go to the make-up room. I couldn't have been any further out of my comfort zone.

Thankfully, everything went well and I needn't have been so scared. I'm passionate about the young people we work with at XLP and although I might not have used the same language as some of the politicians, I felt I was able to articulate what we see young people going through and how we think they can be helped. It was amazing to have a room full of politicians asking what I've learned from my work and how I think they can serve young people better.

After the main stage meeting I was asked to speak at two fringe meetings, one about family breakdown and another on gangs, with Iain Duncan Smith and Richard Taylor (father of Damilola Taylor, who was killed near my home in Peckham). Whilst I had been worried I wouldn't know enough long words to sound clever, people were telling me it was refreshing to hear from someone who works on the ground. The response was amazingly positive. Politicians were telling me they wanted to find out more about what we've seen at XLP and to talk to us about how their policies might work out in reality. Despite my fears, they didn't reject everything I said because I didn't have a degree in youth work or a PhD in politics. People thought my opinion was valid because my team and I had fifteen years' experience of working in the inner city, getting our hands dirty and trying to serve people as best we could.

Tony Campolo said:

> *I contend that Christians will only have authority if they first serve the needs of others in sacrificial ways, especially the poor and the oppressed. When those who hold power witness how Christians live out love – meeting the needs of others and binding up the wounds of those hurting on society's wayside – Christians will earn the authority to speak.*[1]

Never has that been as true as in the case of Mother Teresa. She had no political standing, no power in a worldly sense, yet she addressed world leaders and they sat up and took notice. Her voice continues to be heard across the world, long after her death, because of the integrity in her life. She made heard the plight and the needs of thousands who would never have the opportunity to be heard otherwise. She did what the Bible calls "giving a voice to the voiceless" (Proverbs 31:8).

This is part of our calling too. We're not just called to deal with the results of poverty and pain, but to speak out against the things that lead people into poverty and pain in the first place. Only if we speak out against the injustices in our world and take on the systems that underpin them can we ever hope to see long-term change. As Martin Luther King said:

> *We are called to play the Good Samaritan on life's roadside... but one day we must come and see that the whole Jericho road must be transformed so that men and women will not be constantly beaten and robbed. True compassion is more*

*than flinging a coin to a beggar. It comes to see
that a system that produces beggars needs to be
repaved. We are called to be the Good Samaritan,
but after you lift so many people out of the ditch
you start to ask, maybe the whole road to Jericho
needs to be repaved.[2]*

Often, alleviating pain and poverty is less difficult in many ways
than rooting out and addressing the drivers that cause the pain
and poverty in the first place. Measures to help with the former
are obvious and draw upon our sense of compassion for others.
Measures to overcome the latter often mean challenging
injustice at a political and systemic level in societies that often
favour the wealthy and the powerful – a complicated and
daunting undertaking. But if we read the Bible there is no way
we can escape God's desire for us to be seekers of justice – it's
supposed to be part of our DNA. The words of Isaiah 1:17 are
just one example of God imploring his people to do what he
asks of them:

*Learn to do right! Seek justice,
Encourage the oppressed.
Defend the cause of the fatherless,
plead the case of the widow.*

Most of us would acknowledge that the current systems we have
lead to the rich getting richer, while the poor get even poorer.
We should help the poor, not simply by giving them handouts
but by changing our systems so that they have a chance to
get out of poverty for good. If we do that, they can change
their lives, their children won't be born into poverty and future
generations will have completely different opportunities. If we
keep things the same, we'll be trying to feed their children for

generations to come. The church needs leaders who will take God's values into politics and bring change for those who can't argue for change themselves. We have to be willing to take on those social, political and business structures whose systems aren't just. Desmond Tutu said: "As Christians, we need to not just be pulling the drowning bodies out of the river, we need to be going upstream to find out who is pushing them in."[3]

The reality is that more kids die every day from preventable diseases than die in terrorist attacks, but this doesn't receive anywhere near the same amount of news coverage. There are no headlines, no big memorial services, so sometimes we fail to act to stop these crises. AIDS is a classic example. In the 1980s it became big news because it had just been diagnosed. Now more than 40 million people around the world are HIV positive, with 35 million known cases since 2005 in Africa alone. There are 12 million children in the world who have lost one or both their parents to AIDS. When was the last time you saw that in the news? We have to remember we're not just talking about statistics, we're talking about real people who are dying when they shouldn't be. If any of us were face to face with someone who was dying but we knew that there was medicine available to help them, wouldn't we do anything in our power to get that medicine to them? The reality is, people die needless deaths every day because they live in a country where the right drugs aren't available. The drugs exist, their lives could be saved, but lack of money means they won't be given them. Can you imagine explaining that to someone drawing their last breaths? Or justifying it to a parent who has just had to bury their child? It's unthinkable, yet that's the reality of what happens in our world.

When Bono spoke at an "Africare" dinner in Washington, addressing 1,500 political and media leaders, he said:

*I think that God is on his knees to us, to the
church. God is waiting for us to turn around this
super-tanker of indifference... waiting for us to
recognize that distance can no longer decide who
is our neighbour. We can't choose the benefits of
globalization without some of the responsibilities,
and we should remind ourselves that "love thy
neighbour" is not advice, it's a command.*[4]

A way into politics

It can seem a bit daunting to "get into politics", but it's not
as hard as it might seem. Even knowing our local politician
and praying for them is a great place to start. Not that long
ago I was leading a prayer time about politics for a group of
churches and suggested we get into groups and pray for our
local councillor. People started looking uncomfortable and I
realized they didn't know who their local councillor was. As I
thought about it, I realized I didn't either. It was a wake-up call
and a challenge for me; we're supposed to pray for "all those
in authority" (1 Timothy 2:2), but how can we do that when
we don't even know who they are? How can we make informed
decisions about who we vote into power to run things in our
community when we don't know anything about them? Many
of us hold back from getting involved with a political party
ourselves because we don't see one that holds all the same
beliefs as we do, but the truth is there will *never* be a party
that holds the exact same view as ours. If we want there ever to
be one that comes anywhere close, we can only hope to change
that party from the inside out. We have to make do with the
imperfect parties that exist, get involved and help shape them

towards what we think they should be. We can't just sit back in cynicism and apathy, and hope that the change we long for will miraculously come about. Talking about each party's failings in the pub won't change anything. It's when we're willing to get stuck in and take our place in a political party that we can begin to influence the political agenda. Being involved in politics isn't about the big and spectacular things; it's unlikely we'll ever get invited to garden parties at No. 10. The reality is, if we got involved at a local level, we'd be attending regular meetings, dealing with sometimes mundane issues. But what a brilliant place for Christians to be if we care about our communities and want to serve them. When we get involved locally, that's where hope hits the ground running.

Over the years, I have seen two dominant means by which people try to effect change in society. One is by power and authority, where you legislate and tell people what they "must do or else". The second is by influencing people by acting to be the change you want to see, where people follow out of a sense of relationship.

Those with a short-term view tend to favour the former, under the delusion that it will deliver their goals quickly (or at least before the next election!). The Bible tells us that Satan tempted Jesus in the desert by offering him a quick way to power to help him deliver the kingdom of God. It's as if the devil was saying, "Forget the hardship, forget training the disciples, forget healing the sick, raising the dead and setting the captives free. Forget the cross, the pain, the suffering – get what you want in an instant by taking the power. All you have to do is turn stones into bread, jump off the Temple, bow down and worship me. It's that quick and that easy."

But Jesus knew, amongst other things, that this way would never usher in the coming of the true kingdom of God. Jesus chose, for our sake and for love of the world, to be the change he wanted to see in us. He chose to influence us by showing us how we could live with a kingdom agenda. To do that takes time and it takes sacrifice – there is no other way.

As a follower of Jesus, I want to make the same choice he made and choose not to try and grab power but to live a life of influence and relationship. When we operate like this we truly become the prophetic voice and presence of God. As Jim Wallis, commenting on Christians' involvement in politics, states: "a 'faith-based initiative' is much more than providing social services: it is rather, becoming the prophetic voice and force that can and has moved whole nations to turn into a different direction."[5]

At XLP we have often found ourselves labelled by some Christians as "only a social action project", with the implication that we have somehow lost our spirituality and are simply all about "doing good deeds". But this is not the case by any means. We are constantly seeking God's heart, asking for his leading and direction, crying out to him in prayer and hope for those who are struggling with some of the most challenging life situations imaginable, and praising God for the transformed lives and changed communities we often see emerging in ways that we could never have planned or made happen on our own.

Operating like this requires great wisdom. There were times when Jesus seemed prepared to confront the political powers of the day, but there were also times when he chose to walk away, sensing he had to leave things in God's timing. I truly believe we need Christians to be engaging with the political scene, whether at a local or national level. How else can we truly be advocates for the poor, the disenfranchised, and the marginalized? But, if we do engage, then we must listen to God's voice, his plans, agenda and timing, and not be tempted to artificially create an opportunity to launch Christian rhetoric at the world, and we must guard ourselves against Satan's offers of power (often along with money and sex). This is the way of the prophets – such as Isaiah, Jeremiah, Hosea and Amos. This is the way that Jesus calls us to.

The power of positive alternatives

Often politicians are used to hearing from Christians only when they want to protest about something, but as Jim Wallis said, "Protest is good; alternatives are better."[6] Philip Yancey said that politicians complain that of all the letters they receive, often the nastiest ones are from Christians.

Wouldn't it be better if we were contacting councillors and MPs asking them to come and see the projects our churches are involved in, showing them the positive impact that can be made and asking how we can work together? There's a place for letting our views be heard and standing up for the things that we believe in, but our voice can be so much more effective when we take the time to present a positive alternative and embody a different way of living, not just criticizing others.

Politicians are no different from the rest of us in that they respond well to relationship. Over the last few years I've tried to build relationship with any politician who has shown an interest in what we do. We don't have to agree on everything in order to work well with other people and we shouldn't assume we know where each party stands on every issue. It's easy to write people off and make assumptions about them, but we might be surprised to find out how much we have in common.

It's also easy to stereotype and say all politicians are corrupt and only interested in money. The parliamentary expenses scandal did nothing to help that image, but it was 50 MPs out of 600 who were found guilty of fraudulent claims, meaning 550 didn't do anything wrong and don't deserve the same reputation as the others.

Sometimes we think people in government are only there to make money or gain power, but I've met with MPs in the House of Commons at midnight because that was the only time they were free, and yet they still wanted to attend the meeting rather than say they were too busy. I've known occasions where a Cabinet minister has finished work at 6 a.m., taken two hours to sleep, then got back on with the job. These people are desperate to make a difference through politics; they're not in it for what they can get out of it themselves. We can't tar everyone with the same brush but we can try and build relationships with individuals so we understand what they're about, and we're able to make our voice – and therefore the voices of those we work with – heard.

Sometimes we're tempted to play it safe and stay in our Christian bubble. That's definitely been one of the challenges for me. I was used to speaking at Christian events and that had become my comfort zone; I knew what was expected of me and I felt I could play my part. Speaking to a crowd of politicians and people who rarely set foot inside a church was new to me, but God reminded me it's pretty hard to be salt and light to the world if all we do is attend Christian meetings! As soon as we step out of our church sub-culture we realize how alienated we have become from the culture around us. We use our own language in church, so when we try and explain our faith and why we do the things we do to those outside of the church, we realize they don't know what we're talking about. I've been asked to address police officers on the issues surrounding gang violence, to train foster parents on the same issues and to do a Home Office training event for staff. Each time I felt insecure but also privileged to be able to share what we've learned with these people who are also trying to make a difference in the community. I've been asked to take part in public debates with household names and wondered what I could say. Then I've realized that many working in this arena have statistics about problems and issues, but they don't always have the stories of the people behind the stats. That's one of the things we can do – put a name, a face and a story to cold, dry stats; we can help people see the full picture of what's going on.

In 2010 I was asked to go on Radio 5 and debate with a police superintendent who said we should "lock young offenders up and throw away the key"; he was all in favour of bringing back the stocks, and I thought it would be a huge challenge to put across another point of view against him and his experience. I talked about the things I've seen and how much more money is spent on locking people up than on actually preventing crime in the first place. I talked about the fact that the number of people going into custody has increased by 550 per cent since 1996, but this has done nothing to reduce crime figures. I said that prisons were intended to protect us from criminals but also to help those people get back into society; instead they seem to come out with limited options, so re-offending rates are sky high. I had loads of stories, lots of anecdotal evidence gained from working with young people who've been in and out of prison. He had one line that he was sticking to: we should lock people up. It is important that when we do take up the challenge of speaking in public, we research and thoroughly understand the subject we are discussing – simply saying we disagree with something and we should "lock people up" will never win an argument and does not contribute to solving the problem. We need to invest time and energy, engage with a passion, know what we are talking about, and present good, thought-through alternatives – then people seem to begin to listen to us and want to know our opinion and ask for our help.

Doing a live debate is great, as you can be sure of what gets played out on air, but generally working with the media has its challenges and hurdles because you have so little control. I've been asked to speak to the press more as I've become increasingly involved in the political arena, and obviously there is a clear risk. Unless you're live on TV or radio, you have no control over what gets said and whether your words are kept in context. That's one of the things that often makes Christians shy away from media involvement: we're scared of coming across as over-zealous nutters or having our words completely distorted.

When my book *Fighting Chance* was released, the *News of the World* ran an article on it. The aim of the book was to see behind the frightening media headlines around gangs, and see what the real issues are and how they can be resolved. I rushed out to the shops on the Sunday the article came out, eager to see what they'd printed. The headline read: "Trained to maim aged 7". They had taken a small comment and made it the emphasis of the whole piece. They were just looking for a shocking headline and it left me feeling sick. It wasn't that what they said was untrue, just that they'd taken it out of context and made it unnecessarily graphic and salacious. When your name is printed as part of an article, there's nothing you can do to hide from it and that's one thing I've had to battle with. Ultimately I have to trust my reputation to God and remember that the issues we're talking about are the important thing, not if someone thinks I was involved in a scandalous book. Like working with politicians, the resulting press interest pushes me far out of my comfort zone, but I want to provide a positive voice for the people I work with and the church in the media.

We all know the press often take the most scandalous

or doom-and-gloom stories, so it can be hard to put across positive messages. Sometimes you'll succeed and other times you won't. An article in the *Sunday Express* on our mentoring initiative ran the headline "Mentors plan to stop shocking rise in teenage gun deaths", which gave a fantastic and positive message. The media may like to concentrate on despair but it doesn't mean they won't run stories if we're offering them real solutions to society's problems.

The media interviews I've done have sometimes given opportunities for me to speak about my faith without me having to push an agenda. Talking about positive solutions opens many doors and means other people often bring up the fact that I'm a Christian. I was taking part in a debate on Radio 4 on the back of *Fighting Chance* with four well-known authors and as I wrapped up my section, the interviewer asked, "XLP is a Christian charity, isn't it?" I didn't need to force that into the conversation, as the project spoke for itself and it started a conversation amongst the other authors there about the positive influence of faith on community work. We don't need to feel we have to force the gospel into every conversation or situation; our actions can speak very loudly for themselves. I find it hugely encouraging too that a small Christian charity like XLP can provide a voice for the people we work with in so many arenas.

That said, I have found it such a challenging journey to take a few steps into the world of politics. When you have the Deputy Prime Minister and other Cabinet ministers asking you how to help young people who feel on the margins, you feel an awful lot of weight on your shoulders. I'm still aware that there are many people who are more experienced and qualified than I am, and yet God seems to be opening doors, so I'm trying to be obedient. I've spent time wondering whether it actually does any good to be speaking in this arena; is it all talk and no action? Am I wasting my time? Progress seems slow, but over time it's encouraging to see things change. It may take longer than I would have hoped, but the important thing is that we are going in the right direction.

One of the most famous Christians who devoted his life to politics was William Wilberforce. He stood before the British government and argued that people should no longer be bought and sold like animals. For eighteen years he lobbied hard but faced knock-back after knock-back. He knew slavery was wrong, and he didn't stand by and let it happen. He stood up for what was godly, upset the authorities and people with money and power, and he kept going. Eventually, four days before he died, his Bill was passed by the House of Commons: he had been successful in abolishing slavery. Our world was changed and the lives of thousands and thousands of people were saved because of his determination. He never lost hope; he had courage and conviction and he saw his dream of a more just world come to pass. Wilberforce was an advocate for a group of people who had no voice; likewise, we need to speak up for the poor and disenfranchised in today's world. My hope would be that we would be people who listen to God's plan and his agenda and follow that through. In the world of politics there's a lot of self-promotion and people saying what they think will win them votes. We must respond by living in the opposite spirit. We don't need to be hungry for status, or try and grab power and promotion; if we're going to cast hope, we need to model it. We should respond to challenges with humility, live out what we preach and be in it to serve other people, not our own needs.

In 2010 I was given one of the Mayor of London's Peace Awards at a reception in City Hall. Although I knew I'd been nominated I didn't think I had any chance of winning, so was hugely surprised when I did. I was a bit embarrassed and thought I'd keep it as quiet as possible, until I realized some of the young people I'd brought along with me had already started putting it on Facebook and telling their friends. Someone asked me what I thought the award meant to those young people, and I realized what a positive thing it was for them. I was there representing them and their lives, and I think it meant a lot to them that I was fighting on their behalf and that I was being listened to.

I'm still struggling with some of the language of politics and all the elements of it that I don't understand. I'm still trying to get used to the fact that whatever you say publicly, there will always be someone who will loudly tell the whole world you're wrong. I still often struggle with imposter syndrome and feeling as though I don't belong. These are struggles that I carry with me and try to share with God daily in prayer. What I've also come to realize, though, is that these struggles are worth carrying for the sake of the gospel, and if they help me in some way to play my part in offering the hope of the kingdom of God to those who need it, then I count it as gain.

Chapter 11

Heaven and Hell in Trenchtown

When you think of Jamaica, what comes to mind? Long stretches of white sandy beaches, clear blue skies, calm seas and palm trees? Stunning waterfalls, spectacular scenery, tasty food and exotic cocktails? Sounds like the perfect holiday resort, doesn't it?

The Jamaica that I know couldn't be further away from that idyllic picture.

Trenchtown sits in the capital, Kingston, on the south coast of the island and it has been devastated by poverty, gangs, drugs and violence. Poverty and poor education mean many drop out of school without the ability to read and write, leaving them with few job prospects. Family breakdown and death tolls leave around 90 per cent of children without a dad at home. The atmosphere is constantly tense, with regular shootings that have killed hundreds of people over the last decade. The community is divided into small sections, each controlled by a different gang, and in some places there are four gangs in just 200sqm. There is a pervading sense of fear about when violence will erupt and who will get caught in the crossfire. Innocent bystanders are often victims of drive-by shootings; sometimes it's a case of mistaken identity, other times they will be killed as an act of revenge because of a connection with someone who is in a rival gang. Even children aren't safe; they are often used as targets in reprisals. I heard of a house being set ablaze with young kids inside while the gang who did it stood outside and fired bullets at anyone who tried to enter the house to rescue the children.

Life is cheap in Trenchtown; if you want to kill someone you can get it done for £50. If a man reaches the age of thirty-five in Trenchtown he is called an old man. As you drive around you see children as young as eleven or twelve who have access to guns roaming the streets. You think they can't know what they are doing, but then you'll hear that even teenagers are serious gunmen in this town. Bullet casings litter the streets. Burnt-out fridges and cars divide up sections of the community in an attempt to stop drive-by shootings. Buildings are patterned with bullet-holes from all the years these gang wars have been going on. It's not a place many would want to call home, but as I've visited over the years I've found there are some amazing people who choose to stay in that place because they have hope that even somewhere like Trenchtown can be turned around. They see the potential of what people, and that community, can become.

Ms Lorna is one of those people. She was born in Jamaica and on a visit to Trenchtown she met a young boy who would change her life. He looked up at her, tugged on her shirt and said, "Please, momma, give me some food." She felt God say, "If you don't feed him, where will he be in ten years?" So she moved to Trenchtown with a passion to help children in desperate need and to see the whole community there changed.

She started out with no team and no income, just $700 and the desire to help. She had nowhere to live so she slept in her office, but in some ways that was the least of her worries. With the regular violence, Ms Lorna was just as vulnerable as anyone else but she is the most fearless person I have ever met. One day she saw trouble erupting in the street outside her office with two gangs squaring up to each other. Most of us would have taken cover but she ran straight out into the road and stood in the middle of this group of gunmen who were intent on hurting each other. "You young men are too intelligent to start a war here today," she said firmly, but both sides came back with angry retorts. It turned out the dispute was over a stolen jelly coconut, so Ms Lorna said, "There's no way you are going to start a war over a coconut. If you want to start shooting each other, you are going to have to shoot me first." Ms Lorna's courage defused the situation and the two gangs retreated with no one hurt.

Sadly, she's seen many such fights break out since and sometimes people have even turned on her, despite the fact she's only trying to help. None of this has deterred her from wanting to see change in Trenchtown. Hoping to mobilize young people of low social and economic status, she started an after-school club and went on to start a school. The resulting Operation Restoration Christian School has been a massive success. Many pupils couldn't read simple three-letter words and some said they felt they needed to defend their illiteracy, which led to fights and criminal activity. Three years later those same children passed their Grade Nine exams and were accepted into high schools and colleges. For most it was the first time anyone in their family had received such an education. As well as their academic achievements, Ms Lorna said one of the most rewarding results was seeing their self-esteem and confidence grow beyond what any of the teachers had imagined.

Another amazing woman in Trenchtown, who has become a great friend, is Debbie. She grew up in the community and as a young girl desperate for love, she went from one man to another. Guns are the status and power in that community, so she said she'd never date a man unless he had a gun, otherwise he wasn't a real man. Inevitably she started looking after the guns for the guys she dated, keeping them at her flat in case the men's homes were raided. Debbie's life took a dramatic turn when her brother, a peaceful Christian, was shot and killed. She took me to the spot where it had happened, right in the middle of Collie Smith Drive. Her brother had been preaching when a van drove up and someone in it shot him in a case of mistaken identity. It happens a lot in Trenchtown; drive-by shootings happen fast and the gunmen don't slow down enough to make sure they have the right target.

In the midst of her grief Debbie started thinking about what her brother stood for, and she said the love of God broke into her heart. She gave her life to Jesus and has never turned back. Leaving her "gun-girl" past behind, she trained to be a teacher and is now the Deputy Head of a local school. Instead of choosing to go and live somewhere else without the painful memories, Debbie still lives in the heart of Trenchtown, right between two gang territories. Though she works for peace, she still has to deal with the daily reality of a violent community. Just a few years ago her son was caught in the middle of two gangs firing at each other. He saw a baby who was within firing range, so he ran over to move the child to safety, getting himself shot by a stray bullet in the process. The bullet hit him in the back, but thankfully he survived and the baby was unharmed.

Stories like Debbie's give me hope for Trenchtown. When people are surrounded by violence from a young age, sometimes it's hard to imagine how they can find any alternatives, but I've met so many people who have encountered God and had their lives turned around.

Curtis is another example. He joined a gang when he was nine because all his role models were older guys in gangs. With an absent dad and a mum who was out at work much of the time, Curtis was left to his own devices and would stay up all night keeping watch for his gang. At the age of seventeen, Curtis saw his friend killed and he said at that point the love of Christ broke into his heart. Now Curtis is active in the Trenchtown community running various community outreach schemes for young people and helping them realize what they can achieve. He provides a positive role model that he was lacking as a young boy.

A guy called Destruction is another example. As you can imagine from his name, he used to be heavily involved in gangs and violence, but now he runs netball teams for girls. Most of the girls have such low self-esteem that they become sexually active at a very young age. Inevitably, teenage pregnancies are high, and the girls have little hope for what else their future might hold. Destruction is offering hope for these girls, giving them something to belong to, something to help them build their self-esteem, something that might help change their lives.

Prodigal's father had never been on the scene and he was given away by his mother when he was just three years old. His grandmother looked after him but she died when he was thirteen and suddenly he found himself alone. He began to beg for money and scavenge for food, eating anything he could find in the garbage in his desperation. Then he met the Fatherless Crew. What a telling name! The gang looked after him, made sure he had money and food, and gave him a place to belong. Over time, Prodigal became the Don (leader) of the Fatherless Crew but soon found that others rose up against him, trying to take his position of power. One by one the gang were killed, with nine of the original eleven members now dead. When I asked Prodigal about how he got out of that lifestyle, he told me about a local man, Pastor Andrew, who came alongside him. Pastor Andrew would hang out with Prodigal and others, sharing food with them and taking an interest in their lives. He tried to help people get into employment and spent many hours visiting people in their homes and mediating between gangs.

He preached to them about a God of love and he lived what he preached. Prodigal said that getting to know Pastor Andrew gave him someone to aspire to be like and that ultimately turned his life around. He studied the Bible for a year and he is now one of the country's biggest reggae stars.

Pastor Andrew did amazing work, spending time with individuals, getting to know them and helping them find alternative lifestyles. Tragically, a week before one of my trips to Trenchtown, Pastor Andrew was killed. Someone broke into his home and slit his throat. No one could understand why the crime had been committed – a particularly violent one, even for Trenchtown – when Pastor Andrew was so well respected within the community.

Recent wars

My most recent trip to Trenchtown will always stick in my memory. There had been a time of relative peace the year before I arrived, when the killings and attacks had died down.

However, a gang Don had just left prison and wanted to reclaim his turf from a rival gang. Ms Lorna told me a war was brewing between the two gangs, right in the middle of where Debbie lives. Ms Lorna said to me, "Maybe God has brought you here to stop the war; it could be a bloody one."

I was there with Mike, who had been my intern, and it was hard to imagine what on earth two white guys from England from a totally different culture could possibly do to stop a war between two hard-core gangs. We were at Ms Lorna's flat later that day when Debbie called. We heard Ms Lorna shouting, "Duck, Debbie, duck! Get under your bed!" It was clear Debbie's house was getting shot at and our hearts were in our mouths listening to the conversation. Ms Lorna handed me the phone and all I could hear was bullets whistling through the air, then banging against the side of Debbie's flat. "Patrick, are you there? Can you hear them?" Debbie was saying. She went quiet, fearful that the gunmen would hear her. Then she whispered, "Please pray for me, I'm so scared." I mumbled a prayer about God bringing peace into this situation while I desperately tried to think of anything else I could say or do that would help. I was petrified my friend was about to be shot, the reality of the death stats and the bullet-sprayed walls around Trenchtown coming home to me with a vengeance.

Thankfully, Debbie didn't get hit and the gunmen left. We visited Debbie's school first thing the following morning and were so grateful to see her alive and unharmed. Every morning the school starts the day by gathering everyone together for a time of worship; it couldn't have been more different from the bored hymn-singing I remember from my own school days. Everyone was bringing God their all through praise. Despite the fear and violence all around them, they were singing with joy of his goodness and telling him he's the only thing worth living for. To me they were like modern-day psalmists, singing:

> *The Lord is a refuge for the oppressed,*
> *a stronghold in times of trouble.*
> *Those who know your name trust in you,*
> *for you, Lord, have never forsaken those who*
> *   seek you.*
> *Sing the praises of the Lord, enthroned in Zion;*
> *proclaim among the nations what he has done.*
> *For he who avenges blood remembers;*
> *he does not ignore the cry of the afflicted.*
> *O Lord, see how my enemies persecute me!*

Have mercy and lift me up from the gates of
death,
that I may declare your praises...

Psalm 9:9–14

Even though they are surrounded by people who would take their lives, they still choose to worship and praise God. Later, as we walked to Debbie's flat, you could feel the tension in the air as a result of the previous night's attack. Mike picked up what he thought was an empty shell of a bullet. It turned out to be a live machine-gun bullet and he quickly put it down. Mike and I have both been in some pretty hairy situations before and yet neither of us had ever felt as scared as we did that day. It was surreal to stand in Debbie's tiny, one-bedroom flat and see bullet-holes in the shutters where the shots had come in through the window. Matching holes decorated the walls and I couldn't help but picture her hiding under the bed, fearing for her life. We prayed with Debbie and then, as we were leaving, she recognized one of the gang leaders sitting outside her block of flats. To say he intimidating doesn't even come close. There he sat with a huge knife and he looked us in the eyes as we left. Your instincts tell you to duck your head and run, but that's the worst thing you can do: you have to try to make eye contact and say good afternoon. Strangely, I've found these guys to be incongruously polite and they say "Good afternoon" while holding a huge knife.

March for Peace

Ms Lorna doesn't shy away because of the violence. While we were there she decided the school should do a March for Peace to let the community know how the young people feel about the situation all around them. The plan was that at the end of the march there would be a concert, but because tensions were running so high, the artists who were booked to perform felt that a gig that night was too dangerous and they started to pull out. They said they didn't mind doing the gig in the school yard but not in Collie Smith Drive, as it was too risky. Ms Lorna wasn't interested; the whole point was to do this in a very public place to impact the whole community, so she told me to get in the car so we could go and see the Dons. As we drove down the streets she called groups over and told them what we were doing, asking them not to make any trouble that evening. The Dons seemed pleased to see Ms Lorna and to meet us, and they said, "For you, Ms Lorna, no problem. We will tell everyone to keep it down tonight."

The kids in Operation Restoration spent the day making signs for the march saying things like "Give the youth a chance" and "We can bring peace to our community if we come together as one". A group of about thirty of us set off from the school, the kids wearing their uniforms and holding their signs. It's hard to describe how powerful it was seeing these thirteen- and fourteen-year-olds make such a stand in their community. These kids have seen the devastating effect of gangs and violence. This violence is right in their faces. I spoke to one eight-year-old boy, MJ, who told me he'd seen three people shot and, understandably, he'd since been finding it hard to eat or sleep. Can you imagine growing up with things like that happening around you? With such a high level of violence, they often see it much closer to home, too, with many having lost dads, brothers, uncles and friends to the gang wars. These children are some of the innocent victims of crime and they grow up seeing the life being sucked out of their community by violence. They could choose to follow the same path, so to see them stand in the opposite spirit and make a peaceful but powerful demonstration was amazing. There was still a lot of tension in the community but people took notice as the group went past. They sang Bob Marley lyrics as they went and stopped to pray in different places to ask for God's peace to come. To me, that group were bringing a little piece of heaven to earth. They didn't hide away in fear, they didn't meet violence with violence, but they made their voices heard.

In the evening after the march we set up a small stage in the middle of Collie Smith Drive. The road divides the community in two, so being there meant we could talk to both sides of the community at the same time, ask for peace and talk to them about God. I asked Ms Lorna how often they did this kind of thing and she said it was only when we came to visit, which doubled the pressure I felt. As I took my place on the stage, I wondered again what to say.

I looked around.

The women in the crowd were dressed in tiny skirts and revealing tops; everything about them screamed, "Someone notice me. Someone tell me I'm valuable."

I looked at the children, knowing that they should be living the blissfully innocent lives of the young. Instead they knew all about death and destruction.

I looked at the men and saw that many had guns stuffed down their trousers. Everyone in the crowd knew the pain of losing someone to gun crime. They all lived in fear of violence. What could I say?

I took out a Jamaican £5 note and asked if anyone in the crowd wanted it. Every single hand went up. I screwed the note up and asked, "Who wants it now?" Still all the hands waved keenly in the air. I threw it on the floor of the dirty, dusty stage and trampled on it. It got slightly ripped but when I asked who wanted it, they still all said yes. The point I made was that even though the note was screwed up, it hadn't lost any of its value. I told them that even if they felt used, dirty, or trodden on, even if they felt they didn't matter or they had no value because of the things they'd seen or done, it wasn't true. I said that the truth is that each of us is made in the image of God and he loves us and is passionate about us, no matter what. I said I'd love to pray for anyone who needed to know the truth of their value, and loads came forward. Right there in the street with cars going by on either side, many people bowed down and shed tears. They let go of some of the pain they'd been carrying and we prayed that God would fill them with his love and peace. Afterwards there was a huge celebration and joy such as I've rarely seen in Trenchtown. Again it felt as if a little piece of heaven had come to earth. The kingdom of God broke through into the lives of a bunch of people who felt God would never be interested in them, let alone love them.

The devastating thing was that the very next day three people were shot dead on that same road. That's the excruciating reality. We live in the tension of the kingdom "now" and "not yet". One day we might see a little piece of heaven on earth, the next it feels as if we're in the midst of hell on earth. I believe that we're called to love the hell out of people. We don't just offer them the hope of heaven when they die; we do what we can to defeat the hell that exists for them today. There are always so many obstacles when you try to advance God's kingdom on earth, but Ms Lorna is such an inspiration to me whenever I feel disheartened. She's had so many setbacks but she just keeps going. She's had people tell gunmen that she's reported them to the police, which isn't true and could cost Ms Lorna her life, but she refuses to be intimidated. She invests time and energy in people and then they are killed because of their involvement with gangs, but she holds on to hope and keeps going. She lives a selfless life to help others, but still they sometimes gossip about her and betray her. She chooses to love them anyway.

I have travelled a lot to Trenchtown, and meeting the people there and seeing their way of life has had a massive impact on me. My heart has been broken by some of the things I have seen and heard, but overall I have felt inspired by Ms Lorna's belief that change is possible. She is the perfect example that you can't keep hope down. She lives with daily instability and uncertainty but she never gives up. When we are threatened and things are uncertain and unpredictable, we instinctively try to hide and find safety and stability for ourselves. But when we do that, we stop casting hope. To live counter-cultural lives we have to fight against some natural instincts. If we are not careful, the church retreats to the safety of the margins, but in doing so becomes ineffective and ceases to cast hope or change lives.

Ms Lorna sees what Trenchtown could be. She calls into question the reality that she's faced with every day and compares it to the God-reality of what change could come. She can re-imagine Trenchtown as a place where violence isn't the norm, where children don't grow up fearing for their lives and the community isn't divided by gangs. She sees a place where people love, a place where people know their own self-worth and a place where there is hope for each and every person.

For more information on Ms Lorna's work please visit http://www.operation-restoration.org/

Chapter 12

Hope for the Marginalized and Voiceless

A s the work and reach of XLP has grown, we've started working in East London where there is a significant and increasing Bangladeshi population. With only a limited understanding of Bangladesh, its culture, and the Muslim faith of most of its people, I wanted to learn more to help us work effectively with this community. Previous experience told me the best way to learn was to go to the country, so I made plans to visit Bangladesh and began finding out more about its history and why so many people have emigrated from there to London.

Although immigration of South Asians into Britain goes as far back as the seventeenth century, a war between East Pakistan and West Pakistan in 1971 saw many seeking refuge in the UK. The war was fought bitterly for nine months and though reports on the civilian casualties differ, some estimates put them as high as 3 million people. The consequence was that East Pakistan split away from the West and became Bangladesh. Those who emigrated thought they would find career opportunities; instead many encountered language barriers that prevented them getting a higher education or anything other than low-paid menial jobs. They also encountered a hostile reception from some UK residents.

Arriving in the Bangladeshi capital, Dhaka, I found my senses immediately assaulted by the stifling heat, the sights and the smells. Bangladesh is a country of incredible beauty and culture, but the beauty is juxtaposed with tragic and pervasive poverty. It is one of the most densely populated countries in the world, with around 190 million inhabitants; it certainly seemed as if there were people everywhere and each one gave the impression they were in a rush. The traffic was chaos, with six or seven lanes of cars, trucks and rickshaws weaving in and out of each other in a seemingly ad hoc fashion. Dusty streets were lined with stalls selling everything from spices to saris.

One of our first stops was Sadarghat Port, which is an amazing sight. It is one of the largest ports in the world. Every day around 30,000 people use the terminal and some 200 boats leave the harbour, taking people to various destinations in Bangladesh. Some large boats were crammed with people whilst others carried cattle. Countless smaller boats weaved in and out of each other carrying tourists. Like the roads, the system seemed haphazard and accidents were narrowly avoided. The river itself is filthy from the multiple pollutants discharged into it daily. Human, chemical and medical waste from surrounding homes, factories and hospitals flows into the river; the bodies of dead animals and birds are left there to decompose.

We had arrived in the city a few days before the festival of Eid ul-Adha, which is when Muslims commemorate the willingness of Abraham to sacrifice his son. Families now sacrifice a cow in honour of the festival and it would not be an exaggeration to say there were a million cows in Dhaka. They were for sale everywhere on the streets and once bought, families tie them outside their homes until the festival begins. The meat is divided into three parts: the family retains one portion, the second is given to friends and neighbours, and the last third goes to those in need. This festival is extremely important to Muslims, as it is a celebration of Abraham's supreme submission to God and is also a time for visiting friends and exchanging gifts.

While it should have been a time of celebration, it wasn't long before news came through that the country was going on strike the following day, a sign of the political unrest the country is all too familiar with. Protests were sparked by the eviction of the opposition leader from the home she had lived in for thirty years since her husband was killed. Suddenly everyone wanted to leave the area, fearing what might happen, and the streets were even more packed as people tried to get out as quickly as they could. Our hosts told us to stay where we were for our own safety, and whilst the situation felt tense and a few people were hurt in skirmishes with the police over the following few days, the protests passed pretty quickly.

When it was safe to go outside, we were taken to a slum inside the city. As you can imagine, the conditions there were horrifying, with around 12,000 people crammed into the available space. The walkways were narrow and people milled about everywhere. Kids were running around, the vast majority of whom were barefoot and some were totally naked. The structures that housed people were small, flimsy and virtually empty of possessions. With rubbish everywhere and no running water, hygiene was a big problem, meaning sickness and disease were rife. We saw small children defecating on the floor and parents doing their best to clear up the mess without the resources of running water and toilet paper that we take for granted.

Many had come to the slums after their homes had been destroyed in natural disasters in rural areas, but the slums had already been bursting at the seams before these new arrivals. Local charity workers told us that the particular slum we visited was controlled by a gang member who extorted $1,000 a day from the whole community – this was "protection" money. It was overwhelming to try and take in the level of poverty and need.

Estimates place the number of people who live in slums like this around the world at 1 billion. My mind can't even begin to comprehend that as a reality.

There was one ray of light in this place of desperation. We met a couple who said God had called them to the slum to cast hope. They have two very small rooms, one of which they have set up to use as a healthcare centre so they can treat people living in the slum. The second room they have turned into a small classroom offering rare access to education for local children. The couple told me that when they first arrived, people in the slum were very suspicious of their motives and wary of them. They stayed and loved and served the people, even though the first four years were a nightmare. Another four years on, they say the community trusts them and values their work, seeing that they are there purely to serve and to give. I was humbled at their commitment. A slum is one of the hardest environments to be in and yet they chose to be there and committed to sticking with it even when they couldn't see people responding to their work. I couldn't help but wonder if I would have had their determination or whether I would have given up and assumed that, after a few years without breakthrough, it couldn't be God's will. That couple saw the small shoots of grass in the concrete and refused to be discouraged or to walk away. They live and serve a community in desperate need, being Jesus' hands and feet to people who need to know they are not forgotten.

Refugees

The next day we were taken to a place where the situation seemed even more desperate than that in the slums. It was a refugee camp set up to house people after the war with Pakistan. There are sixty-six similar camps in Bangladesh, housing around 300,000 people who are called "stranded Pakistanis". They are not allowed back into Pakistan but have no rights in Bangladesh either. It's over forty years since the conflict and yet these people are still stranded and now a third generation has been born into the camps. It's hard to comprehend what that does to your sense of identity and belonging in the world when you're not a citizen of anywhere.

The poverty in the camps is on a similar scale to the slums, with whole families living, eating, sleeping, cooking and washing in just a single room. Often the kids will sleep in one bed together while the parents sleep on the floor beside them. There is no space and no privacy for anyone in the family. Toilets are communal, with one for about 600 residents. There are a few hand water-pumps in the camp that each serve around sixty families. The water is dirty, meaning diarrhoea, cholera, hepatitis and malaria are common, especially in children, who are more vulnerable to infection.

The camp I visited had buildings so high that there was hardly any natural light able to filter through. By rights it should have been one of the most depressing places in the world but the people living there were amazing at making the best out of a terrible situation and had incredibly positive attitudes considering their circumstances. I was still struggling to see any hope, if I'm honest. What hope could there be for change if yet another generation was being born into this? Not only was the poverty extreme, but the political aspect made the situation so much worse. I looked at the faces of these beautiful children running and playing amongst the dirt and the rubble, and my heart ached, because it's so often kids who are the innocent victims in situations like this.

Then I was introduced to a couple of people who had seen

the desperate situation and decided to move into the area to do something to help. They weren't able to actually move into the camp, so they set up home as near to it as they could. They had to raise their own support funding and, when they first moved to the area, they went hungry for nine days because they couldn't afford to eat. And yet they stuck it out even when friends and family thought they must be crazy. They said they knew they were doing God's will, so that gave them peace.

The couple started training children in the camps to repair TVs (many of the families have a small TV set) so that they could start earning an income. Most importantly, they started school lessons to supplement the two hours that are provided for the kids. All the children they have in their class are doing so well that they are getting "A" grades in their usual class. Again, education is one of the key ways to empower people to be able to solve their own problems and to provide hope and a future for them. One person commented that the future is not something most kids in the camp can afford to think about, but with this couple helping them to receive an education, their future starts to look a whole lot brighter. With things so tough, I asked the couple how they keep hopeful for the people they work with. They said, "Jesus is our hope. If we have him, what else can we possibly need? The highlight of our day is praying for the children in our school; as we lift them to God, we know there is hope for them."

You can't help but feel inspired by people who have a dedication like this to follow Jesus wherever he leads them and to do whatever he tells them. It makes me realize how often I have clauses on my prayers saying things like, "I will do anything for you, God – but can you make it in this area, where I'm comfortable?" We often define success by numbers (the numbers of young people attending our festivals or the numbers making a commitment to Christ for the first time), whereas they seem to define success by relationship. Their aim is to be Christ to people. They don't have a vision document or a five-year strategic plan; those things have their place, but when our plans and programmes get in the way of true relationship with others and with God, then something is going wrong.

I loved the simplicity of what they were doing. If they were working in their own strength they would have burned out long ago, but everything seems to flow straight from their relationship with God. They put into practice Jesus' command that we love God and love our neighbours. It also reminded me of the parable of the mustard seed that Jesus told, saying that a mustard seed may be the smallest of the seeds, but it can grow and become a tree that provides lodging and shade for the birds. The acts of people working in this camp may seem small and insignificant to some, but acts like these have roots of justice and they too can provide for those in need. Sometimes we need to stop looking for the big and spectacular plans and get on with the day-to-day nitty-gritty of loving and serving people in whatever ways we can.

Sharing our faith with our Muslim friends

Similarly, when we think about how we communicate our faith with Muslims, I wonder if we need to let go of some of our agendas. Often people think the best way to approach such conversations is to have a good argument, using all sorts of confrontational apologetic techniques to prove their point and get one over on the other person. Do we want people to know our God just to make them like us because we fear the unknown? Does this really cast the love and hope of Jesus in the best way? In discussions around Islam it's easy to take an "us versus them" mentality, yet Jesus didn't seem to treat people that way. Before we try to communicate our faith with Muslims, perhaps we need to think through our motives. If we start asking questions about the Muslim faith, let's make sure we're asking questions because we are genuinely interested in the answers and what they believe about God and their faith, not just because we want to use it as a launch-pad for our own theology.

When we're forming friendships with those of other faiths it always helps to start with the things we have in common, rather than the things that would divide us. This allows for authentic relationships to develop where mutual love and trust can grow. When we love people genuinely we start to let go of our agendas and lose the desire to win arguments. Instead we seek to fully understand their point of view and feel able to share our own, knowing we'll be listened to. If we feel we need to defend Jesus and the Bible at every turn, we've missed the point. God doesn't need our help; he can handle his own reputation just fine. Religious people get defensive and like to argue the point for hours; people who love just want to present the good news that they have found. People with an agenda just want to share their own opinions and beliefs; people who love are interested in where other people are coming from.

Carl Medaris (a writer and speaker on Muslim–Christian relations) found whilst working in Lebanon that describing himself as a Christian missionary was the quickest way to lose friends. Many Muslims find the idea of "Christianity" an absolute turn-off, whereas they have a real reverence for "Jesus the Christ" (Isa al Masih). In my experience I've met many

Muslims who have a genuine respect for the Bible, prayer and people who have a real sense of commitment and dedication to their faith.

Carl Medaris now simply tells people he is a follower of Jesus and he says that usually, with a little explanation, he finds people are open to discussing and sharing their ideas about faith. As he said, "Jesus doesn't come with bias, prejudice, conflict, or war. Christianity often does."[1] Carl learned to enjoy friendships with Muslims, not relationships he was seeking to build in order to "win them over". He works with many Muslims in Lebanon and on one occasion a Sunni Muslim parliament member told Carl he had no hope for his country. Carl told this man that he was a "hope-broker" who deals in hope. That inevitably begged the question of where he gets his hope from, and this opened the door for him to share about his faith.

As a result of this conversation with this particular parliament member about hope, they decided to host a gathering, once a week, of people from various segments of the community, including politicians, university students, kids, professionals and poor Palestinians. Some are Muslims, some are Christians, others are Druze (a monotheistic sect found mainly in Syria, Israel, Lebanon and Jordan). First they pray for their country and then they have discussions.

They decided to study the life of someone who had made a huge impact on the world and whom they could learn from, and as they discussed who would be good candidates, the names of Mother Teresa and Gandhi came up. Carl agreed they would be great people to study but then one of the Muslims said, "I've got it! Let's study Jesus!" He said, "Muslims like Jesus, Druze like Jesus. Even the Christians like Jesus!" Others started nodding their heads and agreeing. One of the politicians asked if Carl would lead the study at the parliament, so together the group met there and studied Jesus' life through the book of Luke.

Carl says some Muslims are afraid of Christians but many are willing to look at Jesus.

I found this story both inspiring and fascinating. Many of us judge people of other religions without knowing anything about what they believe. Mother Teresa said:

> *I feel called to serve individuals, to love each human being. My calling is not to judge the institutions. I am not qualified to condemn anyone. I never think in terms of a crowd, but individual persons. If I thought in terms of crowds, I would never begin my work. I believe in the personal touch of one to one.*[2]

If we want to reach out to those of the Muslim faith, we must make sure we don't see them as one large group, identified by their faith alone. We must follow Jesus' example and Mother Teresa's wise words and get to know individuals. We must treat each person with dignity, love and grace, and build relationships for the sake of loving people, not just to win converts to Christ.

East London

Although London doesn't have poverty on the same scale as Bangladesh, the East End borough of Tower Hamlets is an area of high unemployment, poor and cramped housing, financial poverty and high levels of crime. Over a third of the population of Tower Hamlets is Muslim. When our team started working amongst the Bengali communities in London, they found that at first people seemed quite closed to the idea of forming relationships. They were wary and confused about our intentions. Yet, just like the people working in the slums in Dhaka, our guys stuck around, turning up every week, even when it was raining. Slowly people softened, realizing they really were there to love and serve them. Friendships were formed and families started inviting the team into their homes.

Joy from our Tower Hamlets team works with these communities and spent a lot of time with one boy, Abdul, who had been in a Pupil Referral Unit because he was a prolific young offender. He was about to go back into mainstream education but had no support to help him catch up with the schooling he had missed, so Joy agreed to tutor him. As part of her tutoring sessions Joy visited Abdul at home and so got to know his family, including his father, who was evangelical about his Muslim faith. Joy spent time chatting to him about his faith and he shared with her a stunning Islamic book collection. A few months later, Joy saw an Arabic/English Bible that looked just like the books Abdul's dad had shared with her, so she bought it for him. Because Joy knew him and the things that were important to him, she was able to share something of her faith with him in the context of their relationship and in an appropriate way. It opened the way to the two of them sitting down with the Bible and the Koran, talking about the scriptures and their faith.

The team is trying different ways of building relationships that are sensitive to the community. We started taking the XLP bus (which is kitted out with TVs, PlayStations and computers) to the estate but found that many girls in the community weren't allowed to attend the sessions, as boys were present too. We're now trialling some girl-only sessions which also give an opportunity for some of the mums to come along and join in the activities. We're trying not to make assumptions about the Muslim community but to get to know them individually.

We're working with local projects that try to bring different faith groups together over community issues because we want to focus on our similarities before we focus on our differences. In many ways we're just at the beginning of this journey in understanding how to love and serve the Muslim communities around us, but we're determined not to be daunted by the unknown, but to share the hope we have in Jesus by living and loving without agenda.

Chapter 13

Hope for Our Own Lives

When you tell people you're writing a book about hope, they think you must be a born optimist.

I wish that were true. The reality is, at times I've questioned whether I should even carry on writing this book, because hope is sometimes the very last thing I have felt. When XLP started I never imagined it would grow into a charity of the size that it is today, so I never put in any structures that would help me with all that would get thrown my way. To put it another way: I got myself into some bad habits.

Over the years I've repeatedly pushed myself beyond my physical and emotional limits. Seeing people's needs motivates me to do something, so I've often just kept going and kept going long after I should have stopped. When I see heartbreaking situations I am desperate to do something to change them, and every time I come up against the reality that I can't change everything, it's another blow to me. I've often worked for hours then lain in bed exhausted but unable to sleep because of worrying about my team or a child we had come into contact with who was dealing with a terrible situation. I have demanded great sacrifices of myself, putting my own needs way down the bottom of the list of things to think about. I also put huge expectations on myself and constantly beat myself up when I don't achieve them. I find it really hard to let things go and want to give my all to everything. I demanded a huge amount from myself at work and then would demand the same level from myself at home.

I soon became aware that this was a problem. It seemed totally hypocritical to be working to help kids who don't have father figures in their lives and then leave my own children in the same position because I was too busy to spend time with them. One of the dangers in the church is that we try and wear these things as badges of how good we are, how dedicated, how committed and how passionate for God. In reality these are failings, shortcomings that can have damaging consequences for us and others around us. I believe in people taking responsibility, and few things frustrate me more than living in a culture where everyone blames everyone else and no one takes responsibility for anything. It's particularly hard for me when I see the church in general not rising to the challenge and taking responsibility, for sharing the love and hope of Jesus with those in need. But that doesn't mean God is asking me to take responsibility for everything! That's a ridiculous and false sense of responsibility.

Yet I couldn't seem to let go and get myself out of my bad habits. Things started to fall into a pattern of behaviour. I'd work myself into the ground and get myself near to burn-out, recognize the impact this was having on me, my family and XLP, and I'd force myself to have a little rest. But it's a bit like charging your phone for five minutes – you may get just enough juice to last you another day but your battery is nowhere near replenished and working at its optimum. You always feel on the edge of running out of steam. I somehow managed to just about survive in this mode for years. Then a few years ago things started to take a turn for the worse.

Over Christmas my daughter Keziah came out in a rash on her legs and the doctors told us she had a rare condition called HSP (Henoch-Schönlein Purpura). The disease affects your kidneys and bowels, causing fever and sickness in addition to the rash. Twice we were sent to hospital to have her checked over, spending Boxing Day evening sitting with her in her hospital bed, as she was too sick to be at home. Different doctors told us different things. Some said she should be OK, others told us the condition can be life-threatening. You can imagine how helpless you feel when not only is your child unwell, but you're worried for their very life. It took almost eight weeks for Keziah to get back to full health and after just one day back at school she came down with glandular fever, which meant she was very sick for another few months.

One of the ways I try and deal with stress is by playing football, but around this same time I found my knees were getting increasingly painful. I thought it must just be an old football injury playing up, but after X-rays and an MRI scan the doctors told me I have a degenerative knee condition in both legs that meant I needed to give up playing football. I was gutted that I couldn't carry on but the worst news was still to come. Ultimately my knees would need to be operated on and the operation involves breaking the leg and resetting it, so afterwards you have to wear an external frame. The recovery time is up to a year and they would have to do the legs separately, so I started to get really stressed about the idea of that putting me out of action for two years.

As if all that wasn't frightening enough, the doctors said they would wait until I was in an excruciating amount of pain before they would do the operation. They said the recovery is so painful, they have to delay it as long as possible, because without being in agony, I would be wishing I'd never had it done. As you can imagine, hearing this news totally knocked the wind out of my sails. I had all sorts of plans for the future but none involved being in severe pain, having my legs broken, and then being unable to walk for a long period of time. People rallied round and offered to pray, but when there were no signs of healing I put it down to my lack of faith and added that burden to myself.

I was really struggling with all the church politics connected to XLP too; I felt drained and disillusioned. I became sceptical about people's promises. Often well-meaning people would say they would support XLP and help us with our finances, then they'd disappear. It's hard not to grow cynical in the light of that. Plus I had to justify our Christian faith to those outside the church who felt we were too Christian, whilst trying to justify XLP to those inside the church who didn't feel we were Christian enough.

My wife and I decided to take the kids to Center Parcs to get a bit of a break, but when my two-year-old son Daniel went down one of the flumes in the swimming pool he broke his leg. After we'd taken him into the local hospital we realized we'd been in hospital six times in six weeks with six separate incidents. Every type of demand seemed to be raining down on me at once – physical, emotional and spiritual pressures were coming at me from all angles. It felt like an absolute onslaught. Surely things had to start getting easier?

Yet things kept going wrong, with more health problems for Diane and the kids, making me feel even more powerless. Then my dad was diagnosed with bowel cancer. He had to have an operation to remove the tumour but everything that could have gone wrong did go wrong and then some. He was scheduled to be in hospital for just one week but had to stay in for nine and undergo four separate operations. It wasn't even because of the cancer but due to mistakes that were made in his care. My mum and sister are both nurses and a couple of times they spotted problems with his treatment that the doctors had missed – problems that potentially could have been lethal. Every day I'd visit him hoping for better news and to see him on the mend, but every day those hopes were dashed as he lay in bed looking worse and worse. In the space of a few months he lost three stone and looked like a totally different person. Well-meaning people texted him while he lay in hospital, "speaking to the cancer" and telling it to be gone in Jesus' name. I couldn't understand what planet they were on to say these things.

I tried to pray, but didn't feel I was getting anywhere. My head was too full, my heart too heavy; my body hurt all over and I was depressed. I tried to put a brave face on it and just say it was a tough season that would pass, but inside I felt it would never end. The world seemed pretty bleak to me; all I could see was concrete.

So many of us have been in this place where life is confusing. We fluctuate between faith and despair. We question God but then feel guilty for questioning him. We wait for a sign, any sign, but there is none and we feel utterly alone. It's easy to look back in those times to when we first met with and fell in love with God. Everything seemed so much simpler; we were so sure of so many things, and suddenly we feel we're not sure of anything. That's where I was, anyway. I felt utterly hopeless. I began to think of characters in the Bible and the things they had gone through. Noah, who was a complete laughing stock for building an ark on dry land. Abraham, who was asked to sacrifice his own son. Joseph, who was betrayed by his own brothers. Moses, who begged God not to send him to Egypt. Paul, who was shipwrecked and beaten for the sake of the gospel. I wonder if each of them asked at some point, "God, do you really care about me? You're putting me through all of this pain and suffering – why?" All these people are held up as heroes of our faith, but sometimes I can't get my head around how hard life was for them. Even our modern-day heroes, people like Mother Teresa, aren't immune to pain and suffering. She wrote in her diary: "My smile is a great cloak that hides a multitude of pains... [people] think that my faith, my hope and my love are overflowing, and that intimacy with God and union with his will fills my heart. If only they knew."[1]

Personally, I went through various reactions. I beat myself up for not praying hard enough. I compared the pain in my life with the daily reality of my friends in Ghana and Trenchtown, and felt guilty for struggling when they seemed so strong in the face of so much. I questioned whether any of what was going on was because of my sin, so I repented of everything I could think of that I might ever possibly have done wrong. All these things were just vicious cycles that trapped me in their spin, sending me spiralling further down. Then I started getting angry and asking God why I was dealing with all of this. I put forward my best arguments, ranting about how hard I'd worked, how much I'd tried to do God's will, reminding him of the sacrifices I'd made, telling him life wasn't being fair to me. All I wanted to shout was "Why me? Why me? Why me?"

I was having trouble sleeping and, of course, the verse you always remember in those moments is that God gives sleep to those he loves (Psalm 127:2), which never makes you feel any better. Then you're not only exhausted and stressed but you no longer feel like the Lord's beloved.

One night I came across this verse: "You've kept track of my every toss and turn through the sleepless nights,/Each tear entered in your ledger, each ache written in your book" (Psalm 56:8, *The Message*). Suddenly I didn't feel quite so alone. I didn't feel as if I was on my own, and I realized how dangerous feeling isolated is. You feel as though no one understands what you're going through and that no one has ever felt like you've felt. Sometimes in these seasons God is speaking to us, telling us it's not our fault, reminding us he is there and that he loves us, but we seem to shrug it off without taking it to heart. One thing God would always tell us in our moments of fear, pain and suffering is that we are never alone. He is in the confusion with us, he is right beside us and he understands exactly what we're going through.

South African archbishop Desmond Tutu once recounted the story[2] of a Jewish man in a Nazi concentration camp who had been forced to clean toilets. The man knelt with his hands immersed, swabbing and scrubbing away at the filth, and as he did this, his Nazi guard sought to humiliate him further. "Where is your God now?" he sneered. Quietly, without removing his hands from the toilet, the prisoner replied, "He is right here with me in the muck." If only we could all know the truth of that in our times of trouble! Tim Keller says that there is nothing more terrifying for a young child in a crowded place than to lose their parent's hand. Yet he points out that that loss is nothing compared to what Jesus knew on the cross. He let go of his Father's hand in order to take hold of ours, so that we may know that whatever we go through, he is holding on to us.[3] We are never alone. That truth makes such a difference in our times of pain. When we feel alone, we feel we can't cope, and inevitably we start to feel afraid of what's to come. When we know Jesus is in it with us, we feel so much stronger and able to face the future.

At my lowest point, this is what I wrote in my journal:

Hope, what is it really? I hope that one day I will see that light is stronger than the darkness. Until that day I want to be able to see in the dark.

I know grace and truth are stronger than fear and despair.

I believe despite the pain that grips my body that something bigger than I restores my soul.

Hope is knowing there is a bigger picture, hope is the realization that I am never alone.

Hope is knowing that all the thousands of thoughts that confuse me make perfect sense to the one who made me.

Hope is seeing beyond what we are now and seeing what we can become.

Hope is knowing that true love is the most powerful force on earth.

Hope is knowing change is possible when we listen to life's whispers along our way.

Hope is the restoration of everything that gets stolen: joy, health, laughter.

Hope is Jesus, living in us, pointing us to a different way.

Let me love you

During this time, an opportunity came up to visit America on a part-work, part-holiday trip. Diane and I thought it would be good to get away and I was hoping that while we were there God would speak to me about the way forward. People had been giving me lots of different opinions about what I should be doing and where I should be headed, but my head felt foggy from all that had been going on. Much to my surprise, what God said to me on that trip was, "Let me love you." I shook it off; that sounded a bit girly to me. Then someone prayed for me and said that when you run into trouble on an aeroplane you have to put on your own oxygen mask to get your supply going before you can help anyone else. That sounded even worse. God was telling me to stop and get oxygen instead of helping other people?

Slowly the truth started to dawn on me: I was trying to give something to other people that I didn't have to give away.

I must have preached hundreds of sermons on God's love, and yet ironically I needed to be told about God's love again myself. My knowledge of God's love was stuck in my head; I knew I needed to get a deeper level of understanding. In case I had missed the point, God underlined it for me again. When I got back home I went to church and on the news-sheet where the vicar would usually write a little thought, there was instead a poem called "Let me love you".

Of course, being the type of person I am, I wanted instant change. I wanted God to blast me with his love, and change all the situations in my life that felt so wrong. Yet life rarely works like that; things were still stressful, my anxiety was high and my knees and body ached. I knew that God had taken our anxieties, insecurities and pain on himself on the cross, but I realized a part of me wanted to stay in control because there is a vulnerability to letting go. People can be blasé about worry and say, "Don't be anxious, just trust in God", quoting scriptures like Philippians 4:6 and Proverbs 3:5, which says, "Trust in the Lord with all your heart and lean not on your own understanding." These verses are true, but of course when someone is very stressed there is no magic button that suddenly makes everything seem OK.

For me it was a process of letting go, letting God love me and trusting in him. I felt I was letting down the people who wanted me to read those verses and be able to let go of my worry instantly. Henri Nouwen said:

> *Keep saying "God loves me, and God's love is enough." You have to choose the solid place over and over again and return to it after failure... trust that one day that love will have conquered enough of you that even the most fearful part will allow love to cast out all fear.*[4]

I particularly relate to what he says about returning to God's love after failure. When we feel we've messed things up and let God down, that's when we feel our most unlovable, and yet that's when we need God's love the most.

In those moments I have to hold on to the words of Romans 8 and remember that nothing can separate me from the love of Christ. Nothing. Not life or death, failure or success, not funding crises or people's expectations, not the problems of the present or the threats of the future, not ill health, cancer, anxiety, operations, bad theology, being misunderstood or loneliness can separate me – or any of us – from the love of God that is ours in Christ Jesus our Lord.

To receive God's love and try and get myself into a better place, I knew I needed to break some of the habits that I'd been building for a lifetime. I started to have a day off every week (something I'd always intended to do but it often got swallowed by something that urgently needed doing). I also realized I needed some help and support; I needed to be vulnerable with other people and not try to be a lone ranger who takes everything on himself. I started to open up to people about my struggles, got some prayer ministry and also started counselling, which gave me the opportunity to talk things through at a deeper level.

Sometimes pressure and pain has the beneficial effect of forcing us to be a bit more real and honest with the people around us. The church sometimes falls into one of two camps: refusing to acknowledge spiritual pressure and pretending it's not there, or wanting to talk about it all the time and blaming everything on the devil. As C. S. Lewis said:

> *There are two equal and opposite errors into which our race can fall about devils, one is to disbelieve in their existence. The other is to*

believe, and to feel an excessive and unhealthy
interest in them. They themselves are equally
pleased by both errors, and hail a materialist or
a magician with the same delight.[5]

In other words, those who talk about the devil all the time are probably missing the point and those who never talk about him and pretend he doesn't exist are equally missing the point.

When my dad was in hospital it felt so oppressive, as if we were in the middle of a raging battle. After all the mistakes that were made, doctors kept saying, "This has never happened before." They couldn't understand how there could be such a long catalogue of errors in just one man's care. It felt to us as though it was an attack on dad's life and on our family. Battles like these often undermine our confidence in God's goodness and his love for us. The enemy can use these battles and this pressure to wear us down and leave us so discouraged and confused that we start to lose vision and hope.

When I feel as if I'm praying to a brick wall and I'm wondering what God is doing, it helps me to remember what happened with Daniel in the Bible. He puzzled over why God didn't seem to be answering his requests; he prayed for twenty-one days, he fasted, he cried out and prayed more, but still nothing happened. Then he had a vision of a supernatural being who told him God had heard his cries and seen his humility but the Prince of Persia had stood in the way of his prayers being answered. So though Daniel had to wait, God wasn't defeated. He sent back-up in the form of the archangel Michael (Daniel 10:12–13). This is just one of many examples that remind us there are things going on that we don't always see and there is often a battle being fought that we're not always aware of. Through his perseverance, Daniel eventually saw his prayers answered and understood why it seemed as if God had delayed in responding. The Bible calls us to stand against the devil's schemes (Ephesians 6:11). Standing isn't a passive response; it's a response that requires courage. The same passage in Ephesians tells us God has given us armour to protect us. God doesn't want us to be intimidated by the enemy; he wants us to look to him and see that he is greater and he is stronger than anything that might come against us. We need to hold strong to God's promise that his love is enough for us.

Sometimes when things get tough we find it hard to trust God, but this trust is key if we're to get through the confusing and painful situations that come our way. I love the story of the ethicist John Kavanaugh, who visited Mother Teresa in Calcutta looking for answers on how to spend the rest of his life. Mother Teresa asked him, "What can I do for you?" and he responded that he'd like her to pray that he would have clarity. To his amazement Mother Teresa refused. Instead she said, "Clarity is the last thing you are clinging to and must let go of."[6] When Kavanaugh commented that she always seemed to have the clarity that he longed for, she laughed and said, "I have never had clarity, what I have always had is trust. So I will pray you will trust God."

A brave face

To me, this attitude echoes that of David and the psalmists who constantly cried out to God about their enemies surrounding them and overtaking them, but through it all they refused to stop trusting in God. There's sometimes a strange attitude in the church that we need to put on a brave face to cover our pain, as though to share it would be offensive to God. There's no denial in the Psalms of the pain the writers were in; two thirds of the Psalms are laments. But despite their tears, they maintain that God is good, he is worthy of their praise and their trust. They believe that no matter how bad things look, God is working things out. I don't believe all suffering is God's will, but I absolutely believe that he uses any situation to bring good change in us if we let him. I love this quote from *The Shack* (a fictional tale of a man meeting with God in the pain of losing his child), where God says:

> *Just because I work incredible good out of unspeakable tragedies doesn't mean I orchestrate the tragedies. Don't ever assume that my using something means I caused it or that I need it to accomplish my purposes. That will only lead you to false notions about me. Grace doesn't depend on suffering to exist, but where there is suffering you will find grace in many facets and colours.*[7]

I can't say I look back at recent years and think, "I'm really glad I went through that." After all, who wants their child to get ill, or to see their dad sick? Yet I do know that God used the things that happened to teach me more about following him. When the pressure is on, our true character comes out, and it was clear I needed to make some changes if I was going to be useful to God over the long haul.

As ever, God seemed more interested in who I was becoming than in what I could do, and he used the process to refine my character and help me see unhealthy habits I had picked up. It made me realize how often I unconsciously try to do things in my own strength and how instead I need to pick up my cross daily. I want to follow God's plan instead of my own and be more in tune with him so that I instinctively feel able to make the right choices and decisions about my life. I want to be so full of the Holy Spirit that I instinctively know what God is calling me to do. When I face a difficult situation I'd like to know that through discipline and prayer I have developed the right instincts and am able to respond accordingly, rather than needing hours of crisis prayer to discern God's will.

When I played football I was given the nickname "Sniffer" because people said I used to be able to sniff out a goal. My goals were rarely spectacular; I just managed to get myself into the right place at the right time. My coach used to say, "It's just instinct", but of course that instinct hadn't just come about. It had been developed over many years of playing and practising daily. I want to develop my character and my relationship with Jesus in the same way. I want to sniff out what the Holy Spirit is doing so I can get on board rather than trying to persuade God to get on board with my agenda.

Because we don't see the full picture, we so rarely know what is going on in times of trouble. I heard a story about a woman on holiday in South Carolina who came across a 300-pound sea turtle on the beach. The turtle had come to shore to lay her eggs but had lost her sense of direction and was heading to the sand dunes, which would have led to her death. Having covered the turtle in seaweed and poured cool water over her, the woman rang the park rangers who wrapped chains around the turtle's front legs, hooked those chains up to his jeep and then drove quickly through the sand towards the sea. As the woman watched the turtle safely in the water swimming away she said, "I noticed that sometimes it is hard to tell whether you are being killed or being saved by the hands that turn your life upside down." The turtle may have been petrified as it was dragged along the sand, but if it had been left it would have died there on the beach.

That's the way life sometimes seems to me. Often I feel clueless about what God is doing but I have to trust that he will work everything for my good and for his glory, even if I can't see how that will happen. I would love to be able to end this chapter by telling you that God has answered my prayers and I no longer need two operations on my knees, but the reality is, the doctors say I will have to have them in the next few years. Honestly, the thought really scares me and there are still many other areas that I am struggling with too.

In the moments where I can't feel God with me, I try to remember the stories of changed lives and think about the young people who have turned their lives around. I try to focus on friends and family who have struggled with huge issues, yet because of God's grace have come through some incredible challenges. I am trying to let God's love conquer more of me each day, and stand against an enemy that would steal my joy. I find I make good choices for a while and then, slowly and subtly, I fall back into bad habits and start pushing myself too hard and let stress take over. I'm trying to take the right levels of responsibility. I'm trying to remember I am part of a Big Story; that God's grace can change anyone's heart; that I am his child and he promises never to leave me or forsake me.

Some days I do OK; others I get so frustrated with myself and I feel as though I'm back to square one. Day by day I'm learning to give it all over to God, to trust him and to remember that it's OK that I don't have everything sorted. I'm not meant to do this on my own: it's Christ in me that is the hope of glory.

Chapter 14
Hope for Eternity

ope calls into question the present reality and helps us re-imagine the world as God would want it. In Northern Ireland Sister Bridget stands in front of a fifty-foot wall that splits her community in two, but pictures a community united and at peace. Ms Lorna walks down Bullet Alley in Trenchtown surrounded by fatherless kids, and re-imagines a community where peace reigns and families are restored. Pastor Akousa looks at the children of Dampong who struggle to read or write and sees them graduating from university so they go on to live lives they would never previously have dreamed about.

These three women have an astonishing gift of being able to see the green grass growing between the cracks in the pavement. Even more than that, they have hope and vision for a world where the concrete has been completely overpowered and defeated by the grass. They seem to see what Isaiah and John saw when they wrote these passages:

> *I'm creating new heavens and a new earth.*
> *All the earlier troubles, chaos, and pain*
> *   are things of the past, to be forgotten.*
> *Look ahead with joy.*
> *   Anticipate what I'm creating:*
> *I'll create Jerusalem as sheer joy,*
> *   create my people as pure delight.*
> *I'll take joy in Jerusalem,*

take delight in my people:
No more sounds of weeping in the city,
no cries of anguish;
No more babies dying in the cradle,
or old people who don't enjoy a full lifetime;
One-hundredth birthdays will be considered
normal –
anything less will seem like a cheat.
They'll build houses
and move in.
They'll plant fields
and eat what they grow.
No more building a house
that some outsider takes over,
No more planting fields
that some enemy confiscates,
For my people will be as long-lived as trees,
my chosen ones will have satisfaction in their
work.
They won't work and have nothing come of it,
they won't have children snatched out from
under them.
For they themselves are plantings blessed by
God,
with their children and grandchildren
likewise God-blessed.
Before they call out, I'll answer.

Isaiah 65:17–24, *The Message*

I saw Heaven and earth new-created. Gone the
first Heaven, gone the first earth, gone the sea.
I saw Holy Jerusalem, new-created, descending
resplendent out of Heaven, as ready for God as

> *a bride for her husband. I heard a voice thunder*
> *from the Throne: "Look! Look! God has moved*
> *into the neighborhood, making his home with*
> *men and women! They're his people, he's their*
> *God. He'll wipe every tear from their eyes. Death*
> *is gone for good – tears gone, crying gone, pain*
> *gone – all the first order of things gone."*
>
> **Revelation 21:1–4,** *The Message*

Imagining what the world could be like is one of the most uplifting and energizing things we can do. It renews our hope, it gives us a vision to follow, it spurs us on to see what we can do to make that vision a reality. So often we focus on the problems we see around us, the pain and suffering. We need to see those things, but we mustn't just stop at seeing them or we will be overwhelmed and feel hopeless. Instead we must ask God to help us see with his eyes and to give us a ministry of imagination that will help us stay focused and keep hope alive. As we imagine the change that could come, we ask God to equip us to be that change.

My vision is this:

I see a new heaven and new earth.

I see a Bolivian woman, formerly stripped of her dignity by poverty, walking with her head held high and a wide smile on her face.

I see her twin babies, which were malnourished, restored to full health. They run and play, chubby cheeks flushed red as they laugh with their friends.

I see the undesirables, the outcasts, the uneducated, those on the fringes of society suddenly at the centre of a loving community. They are no longer on the outside looking in but right at the heart of a family.

I see school playgrounds in Los Angeles where children can leave by any exit, as there are no gang wars. People of all ages and races enjoy each other's company, realizing they have more to unite than to divide them.

I see a world where discrimination, hatred, anger and judgment have been swept away in a tidal wave of love and acceptance.

I see city streets where no one makes their home in the shop doorways. There is no loneliness or isolation; everyone has a home, a place they belong and an assurance that they are loved.

I see the Shankill Road in Northern Ireland without a fifty-foot dividing wall displaying violent images of the past. There is still art displayed around the community but it symbolizes peace and shows images of Catholics and Protestants celebrating life together.

In this vision my heart no longer breaks for Ghana, because it is a place of great joy. I see Kofi healthy and strong, wrapped in the loving embrace of a mother who is free of her alcohol addiction. The whole community enjoys clean water, safe homes and education; there is no corruption, sickness or disease. The people of Ghana rejoice and live with a sense of hope and expectation about the future.

Across the world I see people who no longer live for the love of power but live by the power of love – selfless lives that put the needs and concerns of others first.

There are no young girls bringing babies into the world just to have someone to love. They don't turn to boys or sex for a sense of self-esteem, because they know their true value.

No boys are drawn to violent gangs because they don't know where else they belong. They no longer need knives and guns, because they don't need to be protected from anything and they have nothing to prove. They no longer live in fear but in love.

I see friends in Asia who no longer need to anaesthetize the pain of their lives through drugs. Their pasts have been redeemed, they are not controlled by anyone or anything. The world is free from addictions.

I imagine a time when no one carries the burden of feeling like an imposter. There is no hierarchy; no one feels unworthy, because everyone is treated with equality and mercy.

The blind can see, the deaf can hear, the lame can walk. There is no pain, no cancer, no need for scans or the crushing weight of anxiety that accompanies them.

The Trenchtown community is united and the scattered bullet-holes are a thing of the past. The men have no use for their guns, so they have been reshaped into tools to work the land. They walk arm in arm with those they once thought of as enemies. The women feel no need to display their bodies to the world, because now they have a sense of self-worth and of purpose.

I see families reconciled that were once wrenched apart through senseless deaths. No parent has to bury a child because of gang violence or a preventable disease.

The Geneva camp in Bangladesh is gone. There are no longer people without an identity, no refugees who feel they don't belong, just sons and daughters of our Saviour and King.

There is no "them and us", no division between anyone. We walk together, laughing, chatting and rejoicing; united as one.

I imagine a time without self-doubt, pain, bitter

memories, or unforgiveness destroying people's hearts. Darkness has been overpowered by light.

And as I look ahead, I see a party begin. No one is held back by injury, pain or disability; they dance without hindrance because of the joy that overspills from their hearts. The sound of singing fills the air, songs of love that are filled with passion and adoration. The former things fade away as every nation, tribe and tongue joins together to praise the King of kings. There is unity, love, grace and joy in abundance.

And in the midst of the throng we look up and see a banquet prepared for us – a lavish feast – where those who once felt marginalized and lived in poverty are the guests of honour. Jesus himself welcomes us in; he is our groom and we are his redeemed and restored bride.

There is a vision worth fighting for; a vision worth dedicating my life to seeing fulfilled. There is a reason to hope for those inside and outside of the church. That is a vision that will both draw the kingdom of God to earth and draw those outside of the church towards their Maker and King. When we re-imagine how the world could be as it is brought under God's loving rule and reign, we realize there is hope without end. It gives us not only a new destination but a new reason for living. We can bring pieces of this new heaven and new earth to our world today. We can share what an eternity with God looks like in a way that makes people desperate to be a part of it. We can proclaim with our mouths and with our lives that there really is no ceiling to hope.

Notes

Chapter 1: The Chance of Hope

1. http://www.bbc.co.uk/news/uk-england-london-11551380 (accessed 24 May 2011).
2. http://www.worldwatercouncil.org/index.php?id=25
3. http://www.savethechildren.org.uk/en/child-poverty.htm?gclid=CP3Oyraa mqkCFQRqfAodsBFUvw
4. http://notalways.live58.org/
5. http://www.timesonline.co.uk/tol/comment/columnists/matthew_parris/ article5400568.ece (accessed 24 June 2011).
6. Pete Greig, *The Vision and the Vow*, Survivor, 2004, p. 104.

Chapter 2: Hope in Bolivia

1. http://www.huffingtonpost.com/rahim-kanani/richard-stearns-of-world- _b_830090.html (accessed 9 September 2011).
2. Desmond Tutu, *God Has a Dream: A Vision of Hope for Our Time*, Rider, 2004, p. 23.

Chapter 3: Hope for Young People

1. Used with permission.

Chapter 4: Hope for Gangs

1. http://www.guardian.co.uk/lifeandstyle/2008/jul/04/women.ukcrime
2. Tim Pritchard, *Street Boys*, Harper Element, 2008, p. 35.
3. The Street Weapons Commission Report, Channel 4, 2008, p. 73.

Chapter 5: Breaking the Cycle

1. http://www.youtube.com/watch?v=rP031DTibQs

Chapter 6: Hope for the Homeless

1. http://england.shelter.org.uk/campaigns/housing_issues/tackling_homelessness/What_causes_homelessness#_edn2
2. http://lapovertydept.org/company-members/lapd-history.html
3. http://www.schoolonwheels.org/about-us/the-need

Chapter 7: War and Peace

1. http://finsburypark.wordpress.com/2008/01/30/postcode-wars-at-centre-of-gang-feuds/ (accessed 15 July 2011).
2. Karl Barth, quoted in Kenneth Leech, *True Prayer*, Harper & Row, 1980, p. 68.
3. Bonhoeffer, *The Cost of Discipleship*, Macmillan, 1959, p. 35.
4. Andrew White, *Faith Under Fire*, Monarch, 2011, pp. 52–3.
5. White, *Faith Under Fire*, p. 51.

Chapter 8: Hope in Ghana

1. Most of the people with AIDS/HIV in Africa are women. See Tony Campolo, *Red Letter Christians*, Regal, 2008, p. 85.
2. http://www.time.com/time/world/article/0,8599,1546100,00.html and http://www.bbc.co.uk/news/world-south-asia-11901625 (19 July 2011).
3. http://live58.org
4. http://live58.org/ For more information: http://www.aaco.org.uk/

Chapter 9: Hope for People with Addictions

1. Jürgen Moltmann, *The Open Church: Invitation to a messianic lifestyle*, SCM Press, 1978.
2. Michael Green quoted by Tom Sine, *Mustard Seed vs Mcworld*, Monarch, 1999, p. 205.
3. Brian D. McLaren, *The Secret Message of Jesus*, Thomas Nelson, 2007, p. 132.

Chapter 10: Hope in Politics

1. Tony Campolo, *Red Letter Christians*, Regal, 2008, p. 40.

2. Martin Luther King, "A time to break the silence", http://holmdelcommunityucc.com/2011/01/011611-martin-luther-king-sermon
3. Quoted by Andy Flannagan, http://www.politicaltheology.com/PT/article/viewFile/10426/7615
4. Bono, remarks at Africare's Annual Bishop Walker Awards dinner, 21 October 2002, Washington DC
5. Jim Wallis, *God's Politics*, Lion, 2005, p. 24.
6. Wallis, *God's Politics*, p. 43.

Chapter 12: Hope for the Marginalized and Voiceless

1. Carl Medearis, *Muslims, Christians and Jesus*, Bethany House, 2008, p. 51.
2. Mother Teresa, *Mother Teresa: in my own words*, Hodder & Stoughton, 1997, p. 99.

Chapter 13: Hope for Our Own Lives

1. Il segreto di Madre Teresa (Mother Teresa's Secret), cited in Bruce Johnson, "Mother Teresa's diary reveals her crisis of faith", The Telegraph, 29 November 2002
2. Archbishop Desmond Tutu, speech delivered before the South African Truth and Reconciliation Commission, 11 September 2002, quoted by Pete Greig, *God on Mute*, Survivor, 2007, p. 279.
3. Timothy Keller, *King's Cross*, Hodder & Stoughton, 2011, p. 69.
4. Henri Nouwen, *The Inner Voice of Love*, Doubleday, 1998.
5. C. S. Lewis, *The Screwtape Letters*, Fount, 1986, p. 9.
6. Drennan Manning, *Ruthless Trust*, SPCK, 1992, p. 5.
7. William P. Young, *The Shack*, Windblown Media, 2007, p. 185.